FINANCIAL TIMES GUIDES

Investment Trusts

Published by
Financial Times Business Information
7th Floor, 50-64 Broadway
London SW1H 0DB
Tel: 01-799 2002
Registered number 980896

Typeset by Infograph Ltd, 37-42 Compton Street,
London EC1V 0AP and ReproSharp, 47 Farringdon Road,
London EC1
Printed by Camelot Press, Shirley Road, Southampton
SO9 1WF
ISBN 1 85334 018 9

First edition 1988

FINANCIAL TIMES GUIDES

Investment Trusts

ANTHEA MASEY

Financial Times Business Information

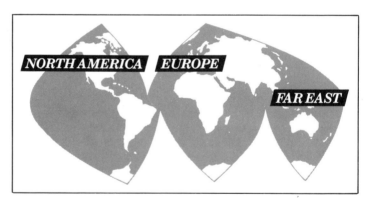

CONTENTS

PREFACE

Until quite recently, I was one of the ordinary men and woman who had
not even heard of investment trusts, let alone understood their advantages.
I stumbled down my own path to enlightenment more by luck than
judgement, through coming to work for the Association of Investment
Trust Companies. Until then, I had spent nine years with a leading building
society, and considered myself fairly well informed in matters of personal
finance and investment. How then could I have failed to have known about
investment trusts?

There must be many more 'ordinary' people who simply do not know
about investment trusts: that they were created over 100 years ago with the
small saver in mind; that they have consistently outperformed unit trusts;
that they are much easier and cheaper to buy than some people would have
you believe.

Not everyone can be lucky enough to work for the AITC! But, with the
help of this excellent book, you can become one of the increasing number
of people who choose an investment trust for their first taste of share ,
ownership. And if the thought of investing in stocks and shares worries you
following the events of October 1987, you can take heart from the fact that
a modest £1,000 invested in investment trusts on 31 December 1945 would
have been worth a handsome £166,425 on December 31 1987.

I confess to being a convert. Perhaps this book will have the same effect on
you.

Lesley Renvoize,
Press and Information Officer, AITC

1 INTRODUCTION TO INVESTMENT TRUSTS

Investment trusts are one of the best kept secrets of the investment world. If you want to invest your money in a wide spread of mainly stock market investments, then investment trusts are one of the cheapest ways of doing it. It's an offer which is hard to refuse, and investors who discover investment trusts are left wondering why they aren't better known and better promoted. This book aims to remedy that situation. It tells you all you need to know about investment trusts, and explains the wide variety of opportunities which exist for making money.

WHAT IS AN INVESTMENT TRUST?

At their simplest investment trusts are vehicles for collective investment. Just like unit trusts or life insurance bonds, investment trusts pool your money with that of others and invest it according to declared investment aims, usually on the stock market. But unlike unit trusts and insurance bonds, investment trusts are themselves companies quoted on London's International Stock Exchange. When you invest in an investment trust, you buy shares and become a shareholder just as if you were buying shares in an industrial company.

Nor are they tinpot fringe investments – quite the reverse. In fact, investment trusts have been around a lot longer than unit trusts and even longer than insurance bonds. The oldest, *Foreign & Colonial*, was formed way back in 1868. The largest, *Globe*, has a stock market value of around £650 million. At the end of 1987, there were some 200 investment trusts and their investments were worth £19 billion.

At this point, the cynic is probably asking why, if they are such a good deal, isn't everyone piling into them. There are several reasons why investment trusts live in the shadow of their better-known cousins, the unit trusts and insurance bonds. The first and most important is promotion. Investment trusts are prevented by law from advertising their shares. And because the shares are bought and sold through stockbrokers, there is no fat commission cheque waiting for the insurance broking fraternity who, as a result, tend not to recommend them.

And then there are the investment trusts themselves. Until recently, many of the big management companies which dominate the industry have exuded an air of staid respectability seasoned with not a small dash of complacency. For a variety of reasons which are explained later, investment trusts are now fighting for their lives, and the one thing they now need above everything else is plenty of investor interest in their shares.

WHO ARE THEY FOR?

Investment trusts are for people who want to invest their money over the medium to long term – say, for more than five years. They are for people who are prepared to take a risk and who hope to be rewarded with a better overall return than if they left their money deposited with a bank or a building society. They are for people who have established themselves financially and who want to start building up wealth by investing in the higher-risk world of the stock market. The three graphs at the end of this chapter illustrate the very respectable performance of investment trusts in comparison with that of shares, unit trusts, building societies, and the rate of inflation over 10, 15, and 20 years.

They are not for people who think they might need their money back quickly. It is important to realise that investment trust shares can go down as well as up. This is because investment trust prices are linked to, although not entirely dependent on, the performance of their underlying investments. You might, of course, be lucky. Many people over the last five years have bought investment trusts and sold them at a considerable profit just a month, six months or a year later. But as Black Monday, that fateful day in the middle of October 1987 when the stock market started its headlong crash, demonstrated, there is no guarantee that this will always happen. If you do buy with the intention of selling within a year or so, you may be disappointed and find you have to sell at a loss.

Prior considerations

Before contemplating a venture into the stock market via investment trusts, or indeed any other medium, it's most important that you first take care of other essential financial matters. Consider the following questions:

• Do you own or are you buying your own home?

• Do you have instant access to an emergency fund deposited with a bank, building society or National Savings?

• Is your family adequately provided for if you were to die prematurely?

• Have you provided for your retirement?

• If you are a higher-rate taxpayer, are you taking advantage of the special tax deals which National Savings offer, such as Savings Certificates and Yearly Plans?

If you can answer yes to most of these questions you are probably ready to start thinking about investing on the stock market.

HOW TO TACKLE SHARE DEALING

The question then is how to do it? Thanks to the Government's privatisation programme, millions of people who previously never dreamed they could invest in shares have now cut their teeth as stock market investors. By the early 1980s, the small investor had been written off as a dying breed. By the beginning of 1987, after the flotation of British Telecom, British Gas, and British Airways, the Treasury estimated that one in five adults owned shares – three times more than five years previously. And with two further successful privatisations in 1987, namely the British Airports Authority and Rolls Royce, and in spite of the stock market crash and the BP flop, the figure is still around one in six adults, according to the NOP.

But it is one thing to fill in the application form for one of these big new share issues where the small investor is almost guaranteed to get some shares and, at least before the BP fiasco, a healthy overnight profit. It is quite another to go that one step further and start buying and selling individual shares for yourself.

Many people who bought shares for the first time in the big share issues, have gone on to discover a real talent for investing on the stock market. These are the investors who are prepared to put in a lot of work reading the financial press and watching share prices. For these people, investment has become an enjoyable hobby.

But it's a daunting prospect trying to find the winners among the 2,500 companies and more than 6,000 different securities quoted on the Stock Exchange. If you are a beginner, you would probably be wise to leave the choosing to professionals.

Buying investment management

If you want your investments managed for you, there are several available choices.

- You can ask a stockbroker to manage your money on a discretionary basis, which means they invest it on your behalf along agreed lines. But unless you are rich – and that means having between £20,000 and £100,000 to invest – no top London or provincial stockbroker will be willing to sign you up on this basis. Anything less is likely to be invested in unit trusts or investment trusts instead.

- You can ask your accountant or solicitor. If the firm you are with is authorised by their professional body to offer an investment service, they may be prepared to do it for you. But it's worth remembering that accountants specialise in doing accounts and saving you tax, while it's a solicitor's job to give you legal advice. They may be prepared to invest your money, but it isn't their speciality, and it's unlikely to get a very high priority.

- You can ask your bank manager. The job is then handed over to the bank's trustee or investment department, but you need at least £25,000, and perhaps as much as £50,000, before they will even look at you. It's an expensive service – the big clearing banks charge a fee of between £6.50 and £10 for every £1,000 you have invested, and that's on top of dealing costs.

- You can put your money in collective investment schemes such as unit trusts, insurance bonds, and investment trusts. For most people this is the best and cheapest way of buying investment management.

If you opt for the latter, it is then a matter of deciding which collective investment scheme is best for you. This book sets out to elucidate the similarities and explain the differences. It punctures the myth that investment trusts are difficult to understand and troublesome to buy. For example, it shows you how higher-rate taxpayers can be better off putting their money in certain types of investment trust shares rather than in the often-recommended insurance bonds. And at the other end of the spectrum, it's not just unit trusts which are making life easy for the small saver – there are now plenty of investment trust savings schemes as well.

FIGURE 1: 10 YEAR COMPARATIVE PERFORMANCE

How £100 invested in investment trusts on 31 December 1977
grew compared with shares and inflation

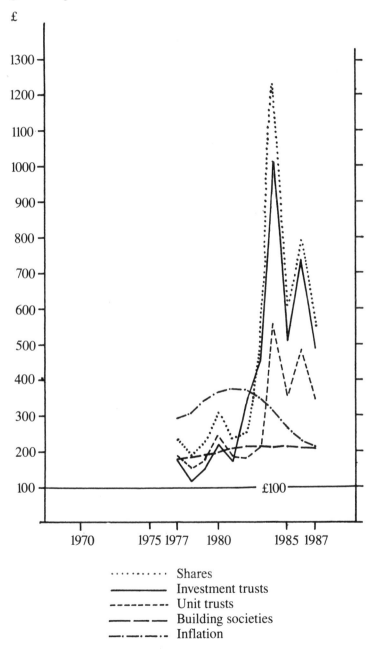

.... Shares
————— Investment trusts
--------- Unit trusts
——— —— Building societies
—·—·—·· Inflation

5

FIGURE 2: 15 YEAR COMPARATIVE PERFORMANCE

How £100 invested in investments trusts on 31 December 1972 grew compared with shares and inflation

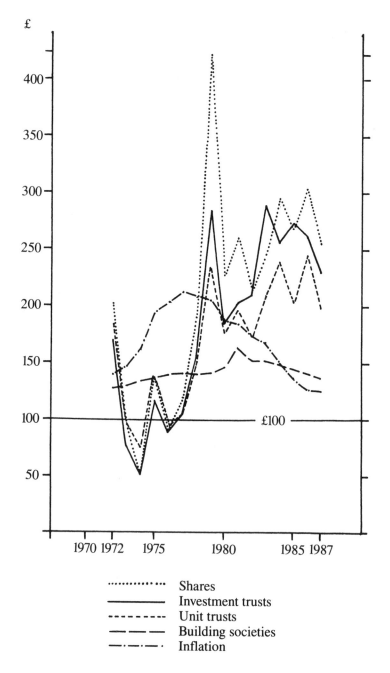

··············	Shares
———————	Investment trusts
- - - - - - -	Unit trusts
— — —	Building societies
—·—·—·	Inflation

FIGURE 3: 20 YEAR COMPARATIVE PERFORMANCE

How £100 invested in investment trusts on 31 December 1967 grew compared with shares and inflation

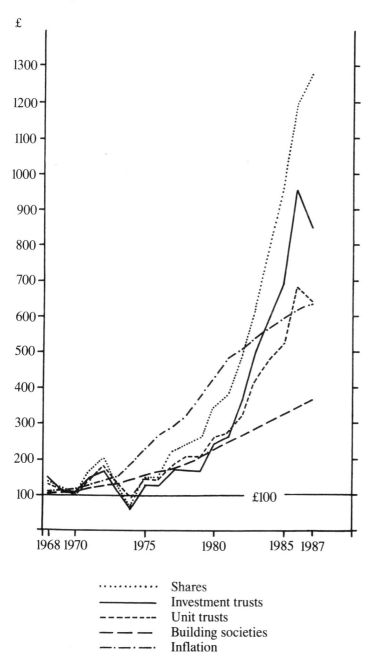

.... Shares
———————— Investment trusts
-------- Unit trusts
— — — Building societies
—·—·—· Inflation

2 WHAT IS AN INVESTMENT TRUST?

Investment trusts are companies quoted on the Stock Exchange. When you buy shares in an investment trust you become a part-owner or shareholder of that particular investment trust just as if you were buying shares in one of our big industrial companies like ICI, BP or Courtaulds.

INVESTMENT TRUST SHARES AND COMPANY SHARES COMPARED

Investment trust and industrial company shares have many common characteristics, but they also have some important differences. Most industrial companies invest shareholders' money in assets which are then used to produce or distribute goods or services. The aim is to make a profit for shareholders, who get their cut in the form of a dividend. Additionally, if the company is successful, shareholders are likely to see a rise in the capital value of their shares as well.

Investment trusts also invest their shareholders' money in assets, but in this case the assets are shares in other companies. The aim is to produce a profit for shareholders, either by increasing the capital value of the underlying investments, or by producing a growing stream of dividend income, or in most cases, by a combination of both.

Like shareholders in other companies, most investment trust shareholders receive a twice-yearly dividend. Companies normally pay their dividends out of profits. Investment trust companies don't make profits as such. Instead, they pay their dividends out of the dividends which they in turn receive from the companies in which they invest.

Determining trust share prices

There are two main factors which influence investment trust share prices. The first is the performance of the investment trust's underlying investments or assets. The second is the market. Like all shares traded on the stock market, investment trusts are subject to the laws of supply and demand. If there are more buyers than sellers, then a share tends to rise, and conversely, if there are more sellers than buyers a share tends to fall. As a general rule, investment trust share prices lag behind the value of their assets, because for historical reasons which are examined in Chapter 3, investment trusts have been declining in popularity.

THE BENEFIT OF INCOME

Stock market investors, whether they buy individual shares or collective investment schemes such as investment trusts and unit trusts, hope that the capital value of their investment will outperform the market as a whole. But what is often overlooked is the fact that if your company, investment trust or unit trust is doing well, it will also give you a growing income in the form of increasing dividends. This contrasts directly with depositing your money in a bank or building society, where your capital is safe, but your income generally isn't. With a bank or building society, your income only increases if the interest rate goes up. By the same token, if interest rates fall you can suffer a drop in income.

The *Foreign & Colonial* investment trust illustrates the point and it would be hard to find a more typical investment trust. *Foreign & Colonial* aims to give shareholders growth in both capital and income from an international spread of investments. On 31 December 1977, *Foreign & Colonial*'s share price stood at 19p and the shares yielded income in the form of a dividend of 3.5 per cent. Ten years later the shares stood at 90p and yielded 2.9 per cent. As the share price has risen, so the yield expressed as a percentage has gone down. But this doesn't show the entire picture. Anyone investing £1,000 in December 1977 would have received a net dividend of £24 that year. Ten years later the dividend on those same shares would be worth £99, an increase of more than 400 per cent.

SPREADING INVESTMENT RISK

Buying investment trust shares often makes more sense than buying individual shares. Investors who buy shares in just one or two companies quoted on the stock market are at greater risk of losing their money than those who spread their risk over a larger number of companies by investing through a collective investment scheme, such as an investment trust, unit trust or life insurance bond.

Moreover, in spite of the increasingly international nature of the world's capital markets, it is still difficult and costly to invest directly in foreign shares. Investment trusts have a long history of investing overseas, going back to the last century when some of the early investment trusts put up the money to build North America's railways. The Japanese stock market, for example, has outperformed all other major stock markets over the last 20 years. And the only practical way for the small investor to benefit from the Japanese economic miracle was through a Japanese or Far Eastern investment trust or unit trust.

PROS AND CONS OF A CORPORATE STRUCTURE

Investment trust shareholders have the same rights as shareholders in any other company. It's the shareholders who own the company, so technically it's up to them to choose the company's directors. Shareholders also have the right to vote on any proposed changes to the company's articles of association and they must be invited to attend annual meetings and any extraordinary meetings. In addition, there is always a procedure for shareholders to call their own special meetings.

Shareholder power

It's easy to dismiss shareholder power as an illusion. But there have been several recent occasions when investment trust shareholders have taken direct action and opposed the managers. In the summer of 1986, a group of shareholders in Ivory & Sime's *Viking Resources*, led by unit trust group Save & Prosper, objected because they hadn't been given the chance to vote on proposed changes to the trust's investment policy. *Viking Resources* had backed North Sea oil in the very early days. The trust had a good record until the oil price collapsed in the early 1980s, since when it had floundered down among the worst performers. In the end Ivory & Sime were able to go ahead with their new investment proposals, but only after calling an extraordinary general meeting at which shareholders voted on them.

Nor was this the only investment trust facing a shareholder revolt in the summer of 1986. *Philip Hill*, an investment trust managed by merchant bankers Hill Samuel, had a poor investment record, partly due to a large long-held stake in Beecham, the drugs and toiletries group. A number of shareholders, led by stockbrokers Barclays de Zoete Wedd, wanted *Philip Hill* turned into a so-called 'index' fund, whose performance would mirror that of the FT-Actuaries All-Share Index. In the end this interesting proposal came to nothing because Robert Maxwell's BPCC made an agreed bid for *Philip Hill*.

Regulatory restrictions

But the company structure also brings its disadvantages. Investment trusts are not able to advertise their wares as easily as unit trusts. There are strict legal rules governing the promotion of company shares which apply to all companies including investment trusts. Investment trusts are prevented from soliciting money from the public with the type of coupon advertising so common to unit trusts. This is one of the major reasons why investment trusts do not get the appreciation they deserve. The problem has receded somewhat in the last couple of years since the development of investment trust savings plans, which have been actively promoted by certain management groups without invoking the wrath of the regulatory authorities.

Investment trust shareholders are now additionally safeguarded by the Government's new investor protection legislation which came into force in April 1988. Under the Financial Services Act 1986, it is a criminal offence for any investment business to operate without being registered either directly with the City's new watchdog, the Securities and Investments Board (SIB) or one of a number of industry self-regulatory organisations (SROs). Most investment trust managers are registered with the Investment Managers Regulatory Organisation (IMRO), one of five SROs. IMRO is at Centre Point, 103 New Oxford Street, London WC1A 1QH, telephone number 01-379 7400.

INVESTMENT TRUSTS AND THE INLAND REVENUE

There are around 200 investment trusts approved by the Inland Revenue under the Income and Corporation Taxes Act 1988. To get approval an investment trust must have a widely spread ownership (i.e. it can't be a 'close' company); it must be resident in the UK; its income must come wholly or mainly from shares or securities, and it must be quoted on the UK stock exchange.

Approved status has important tax implications for investment trusts. If investment trusts paid corporation tax on their capital gains, there would be an element of double taxation if investment trust investors were also liable to capital gains tax on their profits. Tax laws recognise the problem. As a result, approved investment trusts are exempt from paying corporation tax on their capital gains. Investment trust shareholders are liable to capital gains tax in the normal way. But many investors need never pay the tax. All capital gains are now inflation adjusted, and there is an annual capital gains tax exemption (£5,000 in the 1988-89 tax year).

Investment trusts pay corporation tax on their income in the same way as any other company. They must pay tax on any income from deposit accounts, overseas investments, UK gilts, debenture and loan stocks and any income from rent. This is known as 'unfranked income'.

But the income they get from UK companies – their 'franked income' – is effectively tax free. Just like any other shareholder, investment trusts receive their UK company dividends net of tax with an associated tax credit. Investment trusts can then offset these tax credits against the dividends they pay to their own shareholders. Investment trust shareholders get their dividends net of basic rate tax with a tax credit to cover the amount of tax deducted, just like any other company dividend.

Under the approved rules, investment trusts must distribute most of the after-tax dividends they receive from their investments to their own shareholders as dividends. But if dividends fall short of the desired level, they are prevented from cashing in investments in order to boost the dividend payout.

3 THE HISTORY OF THE INVESTMENT TRUST

Today investment trusts are working hard to brighten up their image. It seems light years away from the excitement of the pioneer days at the end of the nineteenth century when investment trusts were all the rage, and the managers were literally pushing the boat out with trips across the Atlantic in search of new investment opportunities.

In fact, investment trusts are not trusts at all – they are companies. They are called trusts because that's how they started life in the 1860s. They only became limited liability companies when their legal status as trusts was challenged in the courts. It may be misleading to carry on calling them trusts, but the habit has stuck and remains an everyday reminder of their early history.

THE BOOM YEARS

The very first investment trust, *Foreign & Colonial*, set out its investment aims in its prospectus of 1868. They were 'to give the investor of moderate means the same advantage as the large capitalist, in diminishing the risk of investing in Foreign and Colonial Government Stocks, by spreading the investment over a number of different stocks'.

Others followed, and were particularly active during the boom years of the 1880s. Some investment trusts went under during the Baring crash of 1890, but most survived, and many of these pioneers are still around today.

By 1900 investors had more than 100 trusts to choose from. And out of the 158 trusts which now share membership of the Association of Investment Trust Companies (AITC), 38 were registered before 1900. Most of the big investment trust management companies have their roots in this period, as the following short histories show.

Touche Remnant

Touche Remnant, the largest investment trust group, manages 11 trusts with assets of around £1.9 billion at the end of 1987. Like many investment trust groups, Touche Remnant began life as the investment arm of a firm of accountants. At the end of the nineteenth century an accountant named Sir George Touche used his investment expertise to launch a number of investment trusts. The investment trust we now know as *TR City of London* actually started out as a brewery. It became an investment trust in 1891 and had a large number of brewery holdings. Other Touche Remnant trusts started life as utility companies. *TR North America*, for example, was known as Continental Union Gas Companies until 1929 when it transformed itself from a holding company with investments in French and Italian gas companies into an investment trust.

There is now no connection between the big city firm of accountants Touche Ross, which Sir George Touche helped found, and Touche Remnant, the investment management company owned since 1974 by the Touche Remnant investment trusts.

Robert Fleming

Today, the Robert Fleming investment management group has a stable of 10 investment trusts worth some £1.5 billion. Robert Fleming, the man who gave his name to this, the second largest investment trust group, was the clerk – what we now call a company secretary – to a firm of jute merchants in the city of Dundee.

The jute merchants of Dundee made a fortune during the American Civil War of the 1860s. The city was awash with money, but there was nothing to spend it on. Robert Fleming came up with the idea of ploughing the money back into the United States using the medium of investment trusts.

In 1879 he started the *First Scottish American Trust*. It's still around today, although now managed by Dunedin rather than the Robert Fleming group. It was trusts like these which put up the money to build North America's railways. The money was normally invested in fixed interest stocks rather than company shares. It was a time of fixed exchange rates, when money could be borrowed at home at three per cent and lent in North America for six per cent.

Ivory & Sime

Ivory & Sime manage 12 investment trusts with assets of £1.1 billion at the end of 1987. They are the oldest investment trust management group still based in Scotland. They began life in 1895 as an accountancy partnership between one James Ivory and one Thomas Sime. As it turned out, James Ivory had a natural bent for investment. He launched his first investment trust, *British Assets*, in 1898, and made a fortune for his investors buying up bankrupt Australian farming debenture stocks. The farmers had defaulted following several years of drought, causing the collapse of a number of Australian and New Zealand banks. What no one seemed to realise, except James Ivory, was that those Australian farmers would eventually pay up.

DECLINE AND FALL

In the United States many small investors lost everything in the years following the Wall Street crash of 1929. Happily, not one UK investment trust went bust during those troubled years. In the early

1930s, investment trusts still put most of their money into fixed interest securities, although by the end of the decade, the shift into equities had begun.

The shift from the small investor to the City

Investment trusts continued to be popular with private investors right up until the middle of the 1960s. But the rise of the welfare state, and the competing attractions of other forms of wealth building, such as house purchase, company pension schemes, life insurance plans and building societies, made it increasingly difficult to persuade private investors to put their money at risk on the stock market. It became accepted that the small private investor was a dying breed.

As the small investor took flight, the big city institutions, the insurance companies and the pension funds found themselves short on the investment expertise they needed to manage this new influx of funds. The investment trusts were happy to fill the gap, and largely switched their promotional efforts from small private investors to big city institutions, with some considerable success.

But as the big city institutions rose in power, size and influence, they started doing most of their own investment management in-house, developing their own teams of investment managers, including those who had the necessary know-how to invest overseas in foreign markets.

The arrival of the split capital trust

In the go-go years of the mid-1960s there was a short-lived attempt to revive the flagging interest of the small investor. In April 1965, *Dualvest*, the first split capital investment trust was launched, followed soon after by *Fundinvest*, which is still around today. Split capital trusts are dealt with in detail in Chapter 9, but basically they have two types of share: capital shares and income shares. If you are looking for capital growth and don't want an income, you choose the capital shares. If you want income, you choose the income shares. This is because split capital investment trusts attribute the capital growth to one class of shares – the capital shares, and the stream of dividend income to the other – the income shares. Split capital investment trusts were an ingenious idea, but on their own they weren't enough to revitalise the entire investment trust industry.

The threat from discounts

By the middle 1970s investment trusts were largely friendless, deserted by private investors and the big city institutions alike. When a quoted company's shares are out of favour, when sellers outnumber buyers, the share price falls to a level where they start attracting buyers again. In the case of investment trusts, this lack of popularity led to the curious situation whereby investment trust shares changed hands at prices well below the value of their underlying investments, i.e. they were at what is known as a 'discount' to their net asset value. Discounts are explained further in Chapter 4.

At this time most investment trust shares stood at a discount to their net assets of at least 30 per cent. The appearance of these discounts was the biggest single threat investment trusts had encountered in their entire 100-year existence. Apart from getting them a bad press, it unleashed a string of generally unwelcome takeover bids, often from big city institutions who could see the chance of buying a portfolio of investments on the cheap.

FIGHTING BACK UNDER FIRE

At one time it seemed that investment trusts would be swept away in the onslaught. But they appear to be made of sterner stuff, and are putting up a spirited fight to win the hearts and minds of large and small investors alike.

It was the British Rail Pension Fund which galvanised the investment trust world into retaliatory action. It showed an interest in the undervaluation of investment trusts by launching a bid in January 1977 for Touche Remnant's £30 million *Standard Trust*. The bid failed – the trust was later taken over by the Prudential – but it sowed the seed of an idea, and it wasn't long before other big city institutions started what they saw as a crusade to unlock those investment trust discounts.

Unitisation

The investment trusts responded with their own ideas, and there followed a whole spate of proposals for unitising investment trusts, which is still continuing. Unitisation is the business of turning an investment trust into a unit trust. It involves winding up an investment trust and offering investors an amount roughly equivalent to the net asset value of their shares in the form of units in new or existing unit trusts. The biggest management groups led the way. In January 1983 Touche Remnant unitised their £42 million *Cedar Trust*. Two months earlier Robert Fleming had done the same with *London & Provincial* and *US & General*.

The threat from 'disguised rights issues'

Just as the investment trust industry was recovering its composure, it encountered a new threat. This time the predators were industrial companies who saw in investment trusts a cheap method of making a rights issue. The idea was simplicity itself. The industrial company makes a bid for an investment trust paying for it with its own shares. The bid values the investment trust's shares at or near the net asset value, eliminating the discount at a stroke. The industrial company gets a portfolio of shares which it then sells for cash which it can use in its own business.

These takeovers became known as 'disguised rights issues', which is effectively what they were. The very first came in 1978, when Barclays Bank bid for The Investment Trust Corporation. But the

15

potential of disguised rights issues was only fully recognised following Electronic Rentals' bid for Fleming's *London & Montrose* trust in June 1982. Others followed, including two from Robert Maxwell's BPCC, first for the £48 million *Bishopsgate* trust and then for the much larger £344 million *Philip Hill* trust.

The advent of specialisation

But unitisation wasn't the only trick which the investment trust world was to pull out of the hat. The early 1980s was a period of massive reorganisation. It was a time when many investment trusts decided that even if they didn't need to change their spots, they did need to define them more clearly. Until then, the majority of trusts offered investment management in its widest sense. Most investment trusts aimed to increase net asset value and dividend income by investing in a wide range of shares, often with an overseas component, usually in the United States. Many investment trust management groups took the view that what investors now needed was more specialist trusts. To support this view, they argued that many of the big city institutions now had sufficient investment expertise to manage the UK content of their portfolios, but some still lacked experience overseas.

Again, it was a move kicked off by the big boys, Touche Remnant and Robert Fleming. During 1982, Touche Remnant converted five of their investment trusts into specialist trusts. As a result Touche Remnant now have three overseas specialist investment trusts – an American, an Australian and a Pacific – and two which concentrate on particular market sectors, namely property and technology. Three of Robert Fleming's general investment trusts were recast as specialist American, Japanese and Far Eastern trusts.

Many people in the investment trust world were casting envious eyes at the unit trust industry, where ever-increasing specialisation looked like the key to keeping the small investor interested. But there were many others who were busy pointing out that the company structure enjoyed by investment trusts provided immense opportunities and that unit trusts operated in an investment straightjacket by comparison. Specialist trusts are dealt with in more detail in Chapter 7.

New ways of investing

Some of the more inventive brains in the investment trust industry now set about exploiting this flexibility, and instead of inventing new types of investment trusts, devised new ways of investing in them.

In October 1982, Scottish investment managers Baillie Gifford launched the first stepped interest debenture stock with an issue of £20 million for *Scottish Mortgage and Trust*. Stepped interest debentures stocks, or STUDS as they are now called, offer an increasing rate of interest – the rate starts low and is stepped up year by year until it reaches a predetermined maximum. In the case of that first £20 million raised by *Scottish Mortgage*, the initial interest rate was 8 per cent. It increases by one percentage point a year until it reaches 14 per cent which it does in 1989, and there it stays until the stock is redeemed in the year 2020. STUDS are discussed further in Chapter 8.

Other variations have followed. In May 1987, River & Mercantile launched a stepped preference share which others have now copied. Here the shares are issued at well below the nominal or par value at which they are to be repaid. The interest rate is stepped also.

Scottish National pioneered the idea of zero-coupon stocks. These stocks pay no interest at all. Instead they are issued at well below the price at which they are to be repaid.

But for the small private investor the biggest breakthrough of all is the introduction of investment trust savings schemes, which allow small investors to deal directly with the managers of the investment trust company rather than going through a stockbroker. The schemes are very similar to the regular savings schemes offered by most unit trust groups. Pioneered by Foreign & Colonial who launched the first savings scheme in 1984, they allow investors to invest a lump sum – the minimum is usually as low as £250 – or a regular amount each month – the minimum is usually £25 – in the investment trust of their choice at a very low rate of commission.

INVESTMENT TRUST MILESTONES

1868   *Foreign & Colonial*, the first investment trust, is launched.

1873   *Scottish American Investment Trust (SAINT)*, the first Scottish investment trust, is launched.

1879   Robert Fleming launches his first trust, the *First Scottish American Investment Trust*, laying the foundations of the Robert Fleming group.

1887   Sir George Touche launches his first investment trust, *The Trustees, Executors and Securities Insurance Corporation*, now *TR Trustees Corporation*, and so starts what is to become the Touche Remnant group.

1890   A number of investment trusts go bust following Baring crash.

1939   Introduction of exchange controls.

1965   Investment trusts taxed on their capital gains following Finance Act 1965.

1965   *Dualvest*, the first split capital trust, is launched.

1968   *Securities of America* is the first public investment trust to unitise, turning itself into a unit trust.

1969   *Alliance* start the first dividend reinvestment scheme.

1977   British Rail Pension Fund bid for *Standard Trust*.

1978   Barclays Bank bid for *The Investment Trust Corporation* in the first disguised rights issue.

1979 Abolition of exchange controls.

1980 Investment trusts no longer pay capital gains tax following Finance Act 1980.

1982 Touche Remnant and Robert Fleming reorganise and relaunch many of their general investment trusts as specialists and unitise others.

1982 *Scottish Mortgage and Trust* issues the first stepped interest debenture stock, now known as STUDS.

1983 Henderson Administration and Ivory & Sime get full listing on the Stock Exchange and Edinburgh Fund Managers are quoted on the Unlisted Securities Market.

1984 Foreign & Colonial start a savings scheme for small investors.

1986 Robert Maxwell's BPCC successfully bids for *Philip Hill*, the biggest-ever takeover of an investment trust.

1986 *Outwich* is the first investment trust to partially unitise, offering shareholders units in a unit trust and shares in *Stratton*, a new investment trust.

1987 *Scottish National* issues the first zero coupon stock.

1987 *River & Mercantile* issues the first stepped preference share.

1987 Edinburgh Fund Managers get full listing on the Stock Exchange.

1987 *Foreign & Colonial* is the first investment trust to be quoted on the Tokyo Stock Exchange.

1988 Shareholders reject reconstruction proposals from Ivory & Sime's *Atlantic Assets* and *Japan Assets* and MIM's *Drayton Japan*.

4 HOW INVESTMENT TRUSTS WORK

There are two important characteristics which set investment trusts apart from other collective investment schemes and which are basic to an understanding of how they work.

- The discount and the premium – or how investment trust share prices don't always match the value of their underlying investments.

- Gearing – or how investment trusts can borrow money to buy more investments.

THE DISCOUNT AND PREMIUM

Most investment trust shares stand at a discount to the value of their underlying shares. Depending on who you talk to, the discount is either the gaping wound which is draining away the very life blood of the whole investment trust industry, or it's their saving grace and biggest marketing tool.

So what is the discount? Investment trust shares are linked to the value of their underlying investments. But because the shares are traded on the stock market, the price of the shares fluctuates according to the laws of supply and demand. It therefore follows that an investment trust share price is rarely exactly in line with the value of its underlying investments, or what is called its net asset value.

Today, most investment trusts stand at a discount to net asset value of around 20 per cent, although some have discounts of up to 30 per cent. Of course the opposite can happen. Occasionally trusts become so popular that the share price rises above the net asset value, in which case they are said to be at a premium.

For investors thinking of putting some money into investment trusts, the discount is just that – an added bonus. Quite simply, it means that investors get more shares and more dividends for their money. Take the case of an investment trust with net assets per share of £1. If the shares change hands at 80p, you are buying £1 worth of assets and their dividends for just 80p, a discount of 20 per cent.

Widening and narrowing

Investment trust discounts can and do fluctuate. If the discount increases to, say, 25 per cent, it is said to have 'widened', and your purchase at 80p has become less of a bargain. Your assets may still be worth £1 but you can only sell your shares for 75p. Conversely, if the discount falls, or 'narrows', to say, 15 per cent, it means that your 80p purchase is now worth 85p and you can sell your shares at a profit.

You only make money out of the discount if it narrows during the time you hold the shares. If it stays at the same level, or worse, widens, then you can only make money if the net asset value of the portfolio increases. Nonetheless, the existence of the discount does mean that investment trusts are at a distinct advantage to other collective investment schemes in that they offer investors two ways of making money: from any increase in the value of their underlying investments, and from any narrowing of the discount.

The danger of discounts

So from the investment trust investor's point of view, the discount is good news. However, for the people who manage them they are a nightmare. Discounts are the equivalent of the Sword of Damocles hanging over the head of almost every investment trust manager in the business.

Up until the mid-1970s the ever-widening discount had the effect of depressing investment trust share performance. This brought them into a headlong clash with their institutional investors and resulted in a spate of unwanted takeover bids from big institutional investors seeking to buy out investment trusts at or near their full asset value, as was discussed in Chapter 3.

And even though the discounts have now narrowed, the threat of an unwanted takeover bid still haunts most investment trust managers. In the heady last days of the 1975-87 bull market, spotting the next takeover target was the favoured sport of all seasoned investment trust watchers. The merest hint that someone was building up a stake in a particular investment trust would send the share price shooting up and cause the discount to narrow.

The history of discounts and premiums

The history of investment trust discounts and premiums mirrors their popularity with investors, as shown in Figure 4 overleaf. In the 1960s, when investment trusts were still popular with private investors, investment trust shares stood at discounts of not much more than 10 per cent.

But as we saw in Chapter 3, by the middle 1970s investment trusts were no longer anyone's flavour of the decade, let alone month. They had been left for dead by small investors and the big city institutions alike. During this period investment trust discounts widened to 30 per cent plus.

The bull market which raged during much of the 1980s plus renewed interest in investment trusts caused the discounts to narrow to between 15 and 20 per cent. This narrowing of the discounts, which many investors had come to think of as a permanent feature of investment trust performance, came to an end with the stock market

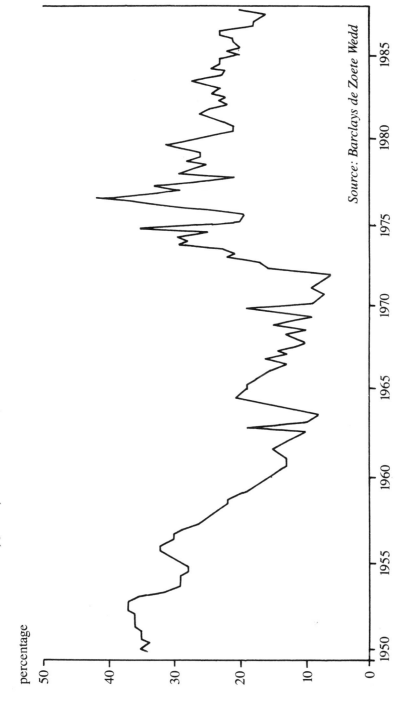

FIGURE 4: AVERAGE PERCENTAGE INVESTMENT TRUST DISCOUNT AT QUARTERLY INTERVALS AT THE END OF MARCH, JUNE, SEPTEMBER AND DECEMBER

percentage

Source: Barclays de Zoete Wedd

crash of October 1987. Take the example of *Foreign & Colonial.* The shares stood on a 33 per cent discount at the beginning of 1977. By the middle of October 1987, this had narrowed to 16 per cent. Two weeks after the stock market crash, the discount had widened to 21 per cent.

Over the last ten years, you would have done better putting your money in a spread of investment trust shares rather than in a similar selection of unit trusts. This is illustrated in Chapter 5. Some of this success is down to the discounts. During this period investment trust discounts came down from around 30 per cent to nearer 20 per cent, after having narrowed to nearer 15 per cent at the height of the bull market. There is, of course, no guarantee that investment trust discounts are going to continue to narrow. And indeed many investment trust experts were surprised by how quickly investment trust discounts widened again once the market started its sharp October decline. However, given the sharpness and severity of that fall, it is perhaps surprising that they didn't fall further.

Figure 5 overleaf shows how *Foreign & Colonial*'s discount has fluctuated since 1982, but how the trend has basically been for the discount to narrow. However, there are investment trusts which have failed to follow this pattern. Japanese investment trusts are a case in point, as Figure 6 illustrates for *Fleming Japanese*. The discount on this trust has widened since early 1986, and was particularly badly affected in the stock market crash. The phenomenal success of these investment trusts over the last 15 years has led to profit taking as investors have worried that the Japanese stock market is overvalued and due for a massive downward slide.

Reading the discounts

The average investment trust discount may be around 20 per cent but this encompasses a very wide spread. At the beginning of 1988, even among the conventional investment trusts, the range stretched from a premium of 6.5 per cent at *Lowland,* to a discount of 30 per cent at *European Assets.* Special factors can throw up even greater peculiarities. For example, *Vantage*'s decision to renounce investment trust status put the shares on a premium of 73 per cent, while the problem of valuing technology investment trusts, with a high percentage of unquoted hi-tech investments, put a trust like *Newmarket* on a discount of 49 per cent.

Always take a close look at the discount before committing any money to an investment trust, but never base your decision entirely on the size of the discount. With some exceptions, it rarely makes sense to back the investment trusts with the biggest discounts. You may have spotted a trust which is destined to be taken over, but you could be in for a long wait, and in the meantime you could have invested in a trust which will really put your money to work.

Always find out why a particular trust is standing at a bigger than average discount. More often than not, it's because the managers aren't doing their job and the shares have few fans. But having said

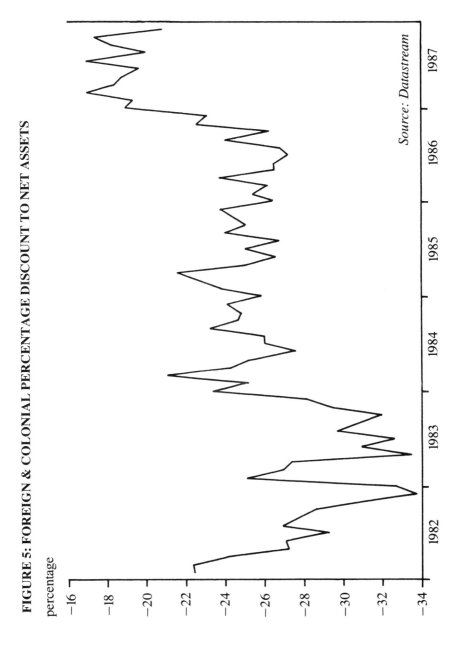

FIGURE 5: FOREIGN & COLONIAL PERCENTAGE DISCOUNT TO NET ASSETS

Source: Datastream

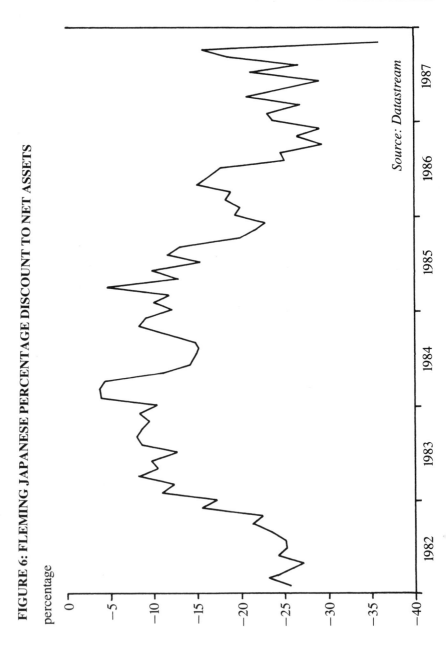

FIGURE 6: FLEMING JAPANESE PERCENTAGE DISCOUNT TO NET ASSETS

Source: Datastream

there are bargains and discounts do sometimes move out of line for no really good reason.

Even over a relatively short period like a year, discounts can fluctuate quite dramatically. The clever investor takes advantage of these short-term fluctuations and buys when the discount has widened and sells when it narrows. For example the discount on *Alliance Trust* fluctuated between 27 per cent and 9 per cent in 1987. There are even more dramatic examples. In the course of that same year, *Lowland*, a small tightly-held investment trust from the Henderson stable, fluctuated between a discount of 13 per cent and a premium of 31 per cent.

There can be bargains among the specialist funds too. These can fall right out of favour when their own speciality is in the doldrums. So long as you are convinced they are being well managed, investment trusts which put your money in particular overseas markets or specialist sectors such as property or energy are worth looking at when every one else is selling and the discount widens.

On the evidence of the 1975-87 bull market, it appears investment trust discounts narrow during the bull market phase of the stock market cycle and widen during the bear market phase. So you can expect investment trust shares to rise faster than average when shares are going up and then fall faster when shares are going down. In other words, investment trust share performance is likely to be more volatile than other forms of collective investment such as unit trusts.

GEARING

'Gearing' is investment trust jargon for borrowing money. Investment trusts are free to borrow money just like any other company. But instead of investing the money in plant and machinery as an industrial company does, investment trusts use it to buy more investments.

In the heyday of investment trusts, when it was possible to borrow money at home at three per cent and lend it in the United States at six per cent, it made sense for investment trusts to borrow money. Nowadays the sums no longer add up so easily. Investment trusts now invest their money predominantly in company shares, rather than fixed interest stocks and bonds. And the income they get from their investments now falls well short of what is needed to meet the interest payments on any borrowings. It is therefore no surprise that, with one or two exceptions, there are now few advocates of gearing.

Gearing increases the amount of money an investment trust has to invest. Shares in heavily geared investment trusts tend to be more volatile than those in investment trusts with few or no borrowings. This is because gearing boosts net asset values in rising markets and depresses them when markets fall.

Take the example of an investment trust with net assets of £1 million. The trust decides to gear up. It borrows £200,000 and invests the money. The market then increases by 50 per cent, and the investment trust's portfolio of shares increases in value to £1,800,000.

After deducting borrowings of £200,000, net assets work out at £1,600,000 – a rise of 60 per cent as against 50 per cent for the market as a whole. Conversely, if the market falls by 50 per cent, the value of the portfolio falls to £600,000 and net assets are worth just £400,000 once the borrowing are taken into account – a fall of 60 per cent.

Most investment trusts pride themselves on their ability to increase dividends each year and investors expect this as a matter of course. It is this factor more than any other which prevents investment managers from introducing or increasing investment trust gearing. This is because the additional dividend income is insufficient, at least initially, to pay the interest on the borrowings, and the dividend paid to ordinary shareholders has to be cut to pay it. This is the kind of stark choice which few investment trust managers are willing to put to their investors.

Gearing through debenture stocks

However, the practice of gearing up investment trusts hasn't entirely died out. Some ingenious supporters of investment trust gearing have come up with new ways of borrowing money. The first solution was the stepped interest debenture stock (STUDS), pioneered by *Scottish Mortgage*. With this type of debenture, the rate of interest starts low and increases over the life of the stock, thus neatly avoiding the problem of having to cut the dividend paid to ordinary shareholders (see Chapter 8).

Others such as *Value and Income* have approached the problem differently. In the summer of 1986 *Value and Income* raised £8 million of long-term debenture stocks. But instead of paying a low initial yield, these debentures pay a flat rate 11 per cent, and the money is invested in high yielding properties. In the early years the yield on the properties matched the interest rate on the debentures. But once the rent reviews start in 1988 there will be a positive benefit to *Value and Income*'s revenue account. At the beginning of 1988, *Value and Income* had equity capital of £22 million and borrowings of £8 million. The managers have said that they would like to boost gearing to a ratio of equity to borrowings of 2:1, which by today's standard is about as high as it goes.

Grahams Rintoul is another advocate of investment trust gearing. When Grahams Rintoul took over *Leda* in June 1987, they changed the name to *GRIT* and introduced an element of gearing with an issue of £10 million stepped debenture stock. The managers' opinion is that if the total return from equities over the long term is greater than the cost of borrowing, then there is no excuse for not borrowing money. They concede that this may mean cutting investment trust dividends, but maintain that most investors are more interested in capital than income growth.

It all sounds very easy. But it is worth remembering that gearing up is essentially a high-risk policy, as the case of *Govett Strategic* demonstrates. *Govett Strategic* followed a policy of taking strategic stakes in companies with a high proportion of borrowed money. It was an aggressive policy for a bull market. Borrowings stood at around 30 per cent of the trust's net asset value at the beginning of the crash. As share prices plunged, this ratio of borrowings to assets shot up and the managers were forced to sell nearly £150 million worth of investments to bring down the gearing ratio. The shares which hit an all-time high of 442p during the summer of 1987, fell in the wake of the crash to a low for the year of 200p, a fall of 55 per cent. By the beginning of 1988 they had recovered slightly to 216p.

Gearing through foreign currency loans

Investment trusts are major overseas investors. Investment trusts which have a big commitment to a particular overseas market often borrow money in the currency in which they are investing.

For example, if an investment trust invests a proportion of its money in the United States, borrowing money in dollars is one of the best ways of managing the foreign exchange risk. In fact any investment trust intent on having an element of gearing is actually behaving prudently when it matches its foreign assets with foreign liabilities.

This is how it works. If you have an investment trust with US investments worth $10 million, and a $10 million US currency loan, those assets and borrowings are worth £10 million if the dollar pound exchange rate is $1 to the pound. If the dollar weakens against the pound and you can get $2 for every pound, the value of those US investments, when translated into sterling, is now only £5 million, a loss of £5 million. However, the value of the dollar loan has also fallen to £5 million. So what the investment trust loses on its investments it makes on its foreign currency loan, and the effect on net asset value is neutral.

Not all foreign currency loans increase investment trust gearing. An investment trust which wants to limit its foreign exchange risk without increasing its gearing, can take out a back-to-back loan. These loans are matched by UK deposits and are made with the sole aim of reducing the investment trust's foreign exchange risk. In these cases the effect on gearing is negligible.

Until the end of 1987, Ivory & Sime's *Edinburgh American Assets* appeared to be highly geared. However, a closer look at the balance sheet showed that the trust's foreign currency loans were backed by holdings of UK Government stocks. Not a back-to-back loan in the true sense, but the effect was broadly the same. In fact, there was even an income benefit. The interest paid on the US currency loan was around 7 per cent, while the trust was earning nearly 11 per cent on its holdings of UK gilts.

5 INVESTMENT TRUSTS VERSUS UNIT TRUSTS

Investment trusts and unit trusts have a lot in common. Both offer investors the chance to have their money professionally managed at a relatively low cost. They do this by pooling investors' money into a fund which is then invested according to certain stated investment aims. There the similarity ends. At the end of this chapter is a brief summary of the differences between the two.

THE POPULARITY OF UNIT TRUSTS

Since the early 1960s unit trusts have been one of the most popular ways in which small investors have played the stock market. In 1960 there were just 51 unit trusts managing funds of £201 million. Twenty years later that number had grown to 493 trusts with £4,968 million of funds under management. By the end of 1987 the ranks of unit trusts had swelled to 1,137 and funds under management reached a record £36,330 million.

The reasons for their success are not hard to find. Unit trusts are relatively simple for the small investor to understand, they are easy to buy and sell, and from the management company's point of view they are straightforward to promote and profitable to run.

Investment trusts share none of these advantages. Compared with unit trusts they are more complex to understand, and before the advent of investment trust savings schemes, much more difficult to buy and sell. There are severe restrictions on how they can be promoted and the management companies say they are not as profitable to run as unit trusts.

If these were the only comparisons which mattered, unit trusts would win hands down. But the closer you look, the more it becomes clear that unit trusts are the Ford Escorts of the investment world – basic and serviceable – while investment trusts are more like BMWs – sophisticated, sleek, and expensive to repair when they break down.

THE OPEN- VERSUS CLOSED-END FUND

Unit trusts are created by trust deed and they have a trustee whose job it is to safeguard the unitholders' interests. A unit trust is a fund of money which is divided up into units. Each unit accurately reflects the value of the underlying investments. If more people are buying rather than selling units in the fund, more units must be created. If the reverse is the case and more people are selling rather than buying, investments normally have to be sold to repay the unitholders whose units are cancelled. This structure is known as 'open-ended'.

Investment trusts are public limited companies traded on the stock market and incorporated under company law. Investors are shareholders and enjoy the same rights and privileges as shareholders in any other company. As we have already seen, the price of investment trust shares isn't always in line with the value of their underlying investments. This is because the shares are traded on the stock market where prices depend on supply and demand as well as the value of the underlying investments. With investment trusts the number of shares in issue at any one time is fixed. This structure is known as 'closed-end'.

Ease of sale in a market crash

There is much argument about the relative benefits of the open-ended structure common to unit trusts and most insurance funds, and the closed-end structure of investment trusts. However,there is no doubt that investors experience fewer difficulties selling investment trust shares when markets are falling sharply as they did in the autumn of 1987.

In the early days of the crash which followed Black Monday, unit trust investors had problems selling their units. Most unit trust managers were almost fully invested, so were forced to sell shares to repay unitholders who wanted their money back. But with share prices falling so sharply most unit trust managers were refusing to deal on the basis of published prices, even if you could get through their jammed switchboards.

The advantage of the closed-end fund in these circumstances is that the amount of money invested is fixed in advance, and no investments have to be sold to repay investors. It means that investment trust managers are not forced to sell their investments during a market crash and small investors normally have no problem selling their shares.

As we saw in Chapter 4, investment trust *Govett Strategic* was forced to sell investments to repay borrowings following the market crash of autumn 1987. This obviously had a very detrimental effect on *Govett Strategic*'s share price and net asset value. But it didn't prevent small shareholders from being able to sell their shares.

There is also a tendency for the discount on investment trust shares to widen when share markets are falling. But again, this doesn't affect the small investor's ability to buy and sell the shares. The crash of autumn 1987 was no exception. Average discounts widened from between 15 and 20 per cent before the crash to around 20 per cent and in the case of Japanese investment trusts to around 30 per cent.

But the closed-end structure can inhibit investment trust managers when stock market conditions are booming and there is a flood of new issues. In these circumstances the closed-end structure can be a straightjacket and the only way managers can participate in new issues is by selling existing investments. Expanding unit trusts – which can be expected in rising markets – have an inflow of fresh funds that they can use to put into new issues.

DIFFERENT CLASSES OF SHARE

When you put your money in a unit trust, you get units in a fund. Investment trusts are much more flexible. The company structure gives investment trusts the opportunity to create different classes of capital – an option which isn't available to unit trusts. It's an opportunity which an increasing number of investment trusts are beginning to exploit.

When most people think of investing in investment trust shares, they think of the ordinary shares. And it certainly remains the case that ordinary shares are the norm, and in most instances are the most appropriate investment for the private investor.

But there are also fixed interest investments such as the traditional preference share which pays the same dividend throughout its life, as well as newer varieties which pay an increasing dividend or none at all and where the dividend rolls up in the repayment value instead. There are split capital structures where one class of shares gets the benefit of the investment trust's capital growth, and another class gets the entire dividend income. There are convertibles – loan stocks which carry the right to convert into ordinary shares. And there are warrants which give investors the right to buy shares at a certain price at some time in the future, but absolutely no income. These classes of share are dealt with more fully in Chapters 8 to 10.

FREEDOM TO INVEST

Investment trusts enjoy a great deal of flexibility when it comes to deciding where and how to invest their money. The most important check on their activities – and it can be a powerful one – is the displeasure of their shareholders, who will be watching to see that their investment trust's stated investment aims are being adhered to. Most investment trusts set up shop with relatively conventional investment objectives. Most aim to provide capital and/or income growth by investing in a spread of shares.

Investment trusts must derive most of their income from shares or securities. Beyond that they are relatively free to invest in whatever they like. However, the Inland Revenue has recently issued new guidelines which restrict the amount of income an investment trust can receive from foreign currency transactions. This followed an investigation into the foreign currency dealings of *Fleming Japanese.*

Nonetheless, anyone wanting to start a slightly unorthodox collective investment scheme has normally adopted the investment trust format. For example, *Alva* invests in unlisted companies which haven't yet reached the stock market, while *Candover* specialises in financing management buy-outs. *London American Ventures Trust* provides venture capital for emerging US companies. There are others too, including several specialist property funds. *TR Property* and *Trust of Property Shares* invest in property company shares, while *Value and Income* has a proportion of its portfolio invested in high yielding properties.

The AITC divides its 158 members into 13 categories and these include five commodity and energy trusts, four technology trusts, 17 which specialise in smaller companies, and 14 with various specialities too diverse to categorise.

Restrictions on unit trusts

Unit trust managers often look with envy at their investment trust rivals. Unit trusts do not currently have the same freedom to invest as investment trusts. The Department of Trade and Industry (DTI) lays down strict investment criteria for unit trusts.

At the moment unit trusts can only invest in securities quoted on recognised stock exchanges. Specialist unit trusts investing only in the UK Unlisted Securities Market (USM) are now permitted, but other unit trusts are not allowed to hold more than a quarter of their portfolios in UK USM shares. Overseas unit trusts can normally only invest 5 per cent of their funds in unlisted securities. This can be boosted to a quarter for shares quoted on the French or Tokyo secondary markets.

Unit trusts are encouraged to maintain a spread of investments, and no single investment can account for more than 7.5 per cent of any unit trust, or more than 10 per cent of any one class of share. Investment trusts on the other hand can invest up to 15 per cent of their assets in any one security.

Unit trusts have had their investment powers widened slightly over the last couple of years, and the DTI has published proposed regulations which will permit them to start investing in other more risky areas such as property, the wholesale money markets, commodity and financial futures and options. However, with the exception of property, restrictions will be placed on the proportion of unit trust portfolios which can be held in such investments.

GEARING

As we have already seen in Chapter 4, investment trusts can and do borrow money which they then use to buy additional investments. This ability to borrow or gear up gives those investment trusts who choose to do it an extra advantage in rising markets. But as we have seen, investment trusts caught with high borrowings at a time when the market goes into decline may be forced to sell investments in order to repay those borrowings.

Nonetheless, this ability to borrow is clearly an advantage, even if few managers take up the challenge. It gives investment trust managers an additional investment tool to help them fine-tune their portfolios. But investors should be aware that the presence of gearing in an investment trust equals additional risk.

Unit trusts are not allowed to gear up their portfolios. They can borrow money, but only to help them manage their exchange rate risks. Unit trusts managers use back-to-back loans, where a foreign currency loan is matched by a sterling deposit. Investment trust managers also use back-to-back loans as a method of managing their exchange rate risk, but it isn't the only method available to them. They are also free to choose other methods of currency hedging, such as buying currency forward, or the use of financial futures.

Unit trusts will soon be permitted to borrow up to 10 per cent of the value of their fund. But they can only do this if they know the money is coming in anyway, for example if they have sold investments and the money is caught up in the settlement pipeline.

BUYING AND SELLING

Unit trust units are simplicity itself to buy and sell. All you have to do is pick up the phone and place your order with the unit trust manager of your choice. The same applies when you sell.

Until recently, investment trust shares have played much harder to get. Investment trusts are traditionally bought through stockbrokers. Many people who are unfamiliar with the workings of the stock market find the prospect of finding a stockbroker, or even asking their bank manager for advice on buying shares, extremely daunting. There is no doubt that the ease with which one can buy unit trust units has been a major factor behind their success.

Investment trust shares are, however, now almost as easy to buy as unit trust units. The big three investment trust management groups – Touche Remnant, Robert Fleming and Ivory & Sime – and many of the small ones now allow investors to buy directly from the managers, thus bypassing the need to find a stockbroker. This way investors can either invest a lump sum or make monthly payments at very low rates of commission. The only disadvantage is that most managers only offer this facility once a month, and not always on their full range of investment trusts.

Comparing the charges

But however you buy your investment trust shares, the costs associated with acquiring them are cheaper than those charged by unit trusts.

Unit trust managers generally make an initial charge of 5 or 5.25 per cent when you buy units. But the difference between the price at which you buy units (the 'offer' price) and the price at which you sell them (the 'bid' price) is often more than this. The calculation is strictly controlled by the DTI, and in theory can go as high as 12 per cent. The published spread is normally between five and seven per cent, but the managers are free to fix their prices anywhere within the permitted spread. And you might just be unlucky enough to buy your units when prices are being fixed in relation to the offer price, and sell them when they are being fixed on the bid price.

Buying and selling investment trust shares should work out considerably cheaper. With investment trusts there is no initial management charge, although there is a spread between the price at which you can buy and sell the shares. The price published in most newspapers is the 'middle market price'. The spread is normally between two and five pence. For example, on 3 February 1988, an easily marketable share like *Foreign & Colonial* was quoted with a 2p spread which is less than 2 per cent. If you wanted to buy the shares, you paid 103p: if you wanted to sell them, you got 101p. Even *Greenfriar*, a less frequently traded share, was quoted at 310p-317p – a spread of 7p, which works out at just over 2 per cent.

There are also dealing costs. If you buy and sell through the investment trust management company, these can be as low as 0.2 per cent. A stockbroker normally charges 1.65 per cent. But watch out for high minimum charges. Some stockbrokers have a minimum charge of £25 or more, which puts up the cost of small transactions. In addition, there is stamp duty of a half per cent each time you buy.

So, to sum up, when you buy unit trust units, between 6 and 13 per cent of your original investment is absorbed in management charges and the bid/offer spread. With investment trusts, the costs associated with buying and selling are less. They can be less than four per cent, and certainly should never be more than eight per cent.

PERFORMANCE COMPARED

Investment trusts have the edge on unit trusts partly because their management charges and the cost of acquiring the shares are less than those associated with unit trust, as shown above. So while an investment trust might have to rise by eight per cent before you could sell it at a profit, the same amount of money invested in a unit trusts might have to rise by as much as 12 per cent.

In addition, investment trusts tend to perform better than unit trusts in a rising market, mainly because the discount tends to narrow when the stock market is booming. On the other hand, unit trusts tend to do better than investment trusts in falling markets because the reverse happens and investment trust discounts tend to widen.

Even so, taking the medium to long term view, investment trusts have usually managed to outperform their unit trust rivals. This was certainly the case during the bull market which dominated much of the 1980s. The crash of autumn 1987 certainly left a few investment trust managers' reputations in tatters: nonetheless, the industry as a whole has emerged intact, and as you can see from the table overleaf, with the exception of the six-month performance figures, investment trusts are still showing unit trusts a clean pair of heels.

Performance of investment trusts and unit trusts compared

£1,000 invested, net income re-invested, as at 30.4.88

	6 mnths £	1 yr £	3 yrs £	5 yrs £	7 yrs £
Unit trusts	1,039	921	1,553	2,098	2,876
Investment trusts	1,002	964	1,651	2,524	3,511

Source: Opal Statistics

DIFFERENCES IN PROMOTION METHODS

Investment trusts have a great deal of difficulty getting their message across to the public. There must be many thousands of unit trust investors who would be equally interested in investment trusts if only they knew about them. The company structure brings investment trusts many advantages, but, as discussed in Chapter 2, it does inhibit their ability to sell themselves. Companies are not permitted to promote their own shares unless they produce a full-scale prospectus, and clearly no investment trust can afford to do this each time it wants to promote itself.

Investment trusts would be breaking the law if they engaged in the kind of 'money off the page' newspaper advertising favoured by unit trust groups. Investment trusts have found several ways round the problem. The AITC does generic advertising on behalf of the entire industry. And since the advent of savings schemes, individual management companies have advertised them without falling foul of the law. But even these schemes cannot be promoted as aggressively as unit trusts. Potential investment trust investors must send in for an application form before they send in their money.

SUMMARY OF THE DIFFERENCES BETWEEN INVESTMENT TRUSTS AND UNIT TRUSTS

Investment Trusts	*Unit Trusts*
Closed-end funds with a fixed capital. In falling markets managers are not normally forced to sell investments.	Open-ended funds - the units in issue are adjusted in line with demand. Managers may be forced to sell investments when markets fall to repay unitholders.
Easy to sell in falling markets.	Can be difficult to sell quickly in falling markets.
Company structure gives investors rights as shareholders.	Few rights. Unitholders safeguarded by trustee.
Structure inhibits managers from taking up new issues.	Expanding unit trusts can take advantage of new issues.
Discounts give investors the chance to buy assets and income on the cheap.	Unit value reflects value of underlying investments.
Can borrow money to gear up their portfolios.	Not generally permitted to borrow money.
Different classes of investment available, such as income and capital shares, preference shares, warrants and convertibles.	Only units available.
Share performance can be volatile.	Less volatile than investment trusts.
Few restrictions on where money invested.	Restrictions on where money invested.
Management and acquisition costs generally lower than unit trusts.	Management and acquisition costs generally higher than investment trusts.
Promotion restricted.	Easy to promote.

6 HOW TO BUY INVESTMENT TRUST SHARES

Investment trusts are companies whose shares are traded on the Stock Exchange. Until recently most people backed away in fear at the first mention of anything to do with shares and the Stock Exchange, preferring the safe and predictable world of National Savings, the high street banks and building societies. The great privatisation issues – British Telecom, British Gas and British Airways – changed all that when they forged a new breed of small private investors.

Nonetheless, it is one thing to fill in a widely available application form for shares in privatisation issues, quite another to then go on to buy and sell shares of your own choice all by yourself.

There are a number of ways of buying shares. You can use:
a) a stockbroker
b) a bank manager
c) an accountant or solicitor
d) a share dealer
e) a share shop
f) if you are buying investment trust shares you can go directly to the management company.

SAVINGS SCHEMES

Buying directly from the investment trust management company through a savings scheme is now the cheapest way of buying investment trust shares – the commission charged is often well below one per cent and there is usually no minimum charge.

The term 'savings scheme' is somewhat misleading. Investment trust savings schemes are not just for investors who want to save a regular amount each month. They are also for anyone who wants to invest a lump sum, and the minimum investment is normally as low as £250.

But there are disadvantages. In most cases, you can only invest the money once a month, and you may not want to wait that long. However, by pooling everyone's purchases and putting a bulk order through one stockbroker, the investment trust managers can negotiate the commission rate, and it's only by doing it this way that the investment managers can charge such low levels of commission. You may find that the investment trust which has caught your fancy doesn't operate a savings scheme, because there are still a sizeable number which can't be bought this way. For more information on how savings schemes work, see Chapter 18.

USING A STOCKBROKER

If you want to feel more in control of your investment destiny, and you want to buy other shares as well as those in investment trusts, your best bet is to find a stockbroker. For a lot of people this is a daunting business. It shouldn't be.

The best place to start your search is, not surprisingly, the Stock Exchange. They now produce an excellent booklet, 'An Introduction to The Stock Market'. It costs £1 – make your cheque payable to the International Stock Exchange – and you can get it by writing to The International Stock Exchange, London EC2N 1HP. The booklet explains how the stock market works, and at the back there is a list of stockbrokers who are on the look-out for new private clients. What it won't tell you is how much commission each stockbroker charges. For this you need the list compiled by the AITC which is available free from AITC, 6th floor, Park House, 16 Finsbury Circus, London EC2M 7JJ. The list was updated in February 1988, but with stockbrokers only recently free to charge what they like, minimum commission rates are changing all the time, and any published list is soon out of date. Nonetheless, the AITC list is still a useful source of information on stockbrokers and what they have on offer if you want to put your money in investment trusts.

Levels of service available

Most stockbrokers offer several levels of service. If all you want is someone who efficiently buys and sells shares on your behalf, go for a no-frills dealing service. Once accepted as creditworthy, you can instruct your stockbroker over the telephone. But if you want to deal in small quantities of shares make sure you know your stockbroker's minimum commission charge. And don't expect anyone to hold your hand. With these cheap and cheerful dealing-only services, the competition is fierce and the commission rates are pared fine. There is not much left over to pay for the niceties.

If you don't feel entirely confident about which shares to buy and when to sell, opt for a stockbroker who is prepared to give you advice. This can be anything from cosy chats over the phone, to receiving circulars and share recommendations through the post. But be warned – many stockbrokers are reluctant to put this kind of time and money into private clients unless they invest at least £10,000 through the firm. On the other hand, there are stockbrokers, mainly outside London, who say they are happy to advise all their private clients regardless of how much money they have to invest, but don't expect the kind of professionalism you would get from a big London firm with its own research department.

If you want to invest in equities, but don't want the bother of deciding which ones to buy, you can hand your money over to a stockbroker and ask them to do it for you on what is called a 'discretionary' basis. Again, there are stockbrokers who say they are willing to manage any amount on this basis. But in practice, most stockbrokers would find it difficult to construct a well-balanced spread of shares unless they had at least £20,000 to play with.

Dealing costs

Since Big Bang in October 1986, stockbrokers have been free to charge what they like in commission. For small deals, most stockbrokers have stuck to the old commission rate of 1.65 per cent. For most private investors, especially those who want to deal in amounts under £1,000, the most important figure to watch is the minimum commission charge. This varies from firm to firm, and sometimes varies with the level of service too. Some firms charge as little as £8, others as much as £50.

So it doesn't always makes sense to go for the stockbroker with the cheapest actual commission rate. If you want to buy £500 worth of shares, you pay less commission if you go to a stockbroker who charges commission of 1.65 per cent, but who imposes a minimum charge of £10, rather than a firm which charges 1.5 per cent commission but imposes a minimum charge of £20. In both cases, the actual commission comes to less than the minimum charge, so the firm charging just £10 works out cheaper.

Brokers outside London have fewer overheads, and thanks to their lower costs, they can keep their charges down. If all you are after is a cheap no-frills dealing service, you are likely to do better choosing a provincial broker rather than a firm based in the City.

What top advice costs

If you are looking for a stockbroker who knows all about investment trusts, the AITC booklet can steer you in the right direction. What it doesn't tell you is how good that advice is. For this you need the results of the ranking of UK investment analysts prepared by Extel Financial. Every year Extel ask the big City institutions which stockbrokers' analysts are doing the best job.

In the field of investment trusts, three firms reign supreme. They are NatWest Wood Mackenzie, James Capel and Warburg Securities. To get the benefit of their advice you need to be a client, and to be a client of one of these firms you need to be well-heeled.

Since they were taken over by NatWest Bank, NatWest Wood Mackenzie no longer have a private client department. However, private clients of NatWest Stockbrokers do have access to NatWest Wood Mackenzie investment trust research, but you would need to invest at least £40,000 in investment trusts before they would admit you to their advisory service. And then they would charge you a fee of £250 a year, on top of commission of 1.5 per cent with a minimum of £30 on each transaction.

James Capel are even more exclusive. You need £200,000 before James Capel will offer you their full portfolio advisory service, although they are happy to advise on single share purchases above £5,000. Given the minimum commission charge, anything less would work out very expensive. James Capel charge commission of 1.65 per cent, but the minimum is a mighty £50.

Of the big three, Warburg Securities are the most exclusive. You need to invest £300,000 before you can benefit from their advice.

Barclays de Zoete Wedd head up the second division, but this is another of the City's more exclusive private client departments. Here you need £250,000 before you get the benefit of their investment trust advice. However, if you are very persistent and know what to ask for, you may be able to get access to Barclays de Zoete Wedd's research through Barclayshare, the advice service available from Barclays Bank. The service costs £15 a quarter on top of any dealing costs. For this you get a monthly investment advice sheet, which regularly recommends investment trusts, and you can telephone Barclayshare for advice.

OTHER SOURCES OF ADVICE

There are five specialist investment trust advisory services, but again they aren't cheap. These are for investors who want to build up a portfolio of investment trust shares, but don't want the worry of choosing which ones to buy.

Investment trust managers Touche Remnant operate a scheme for people with at least £20,000 to invest. Under the rules of the scheme Touche Remnant don't invest more than a third in their own investment trusts without the written permission of the client. There is an initial setting up charge of £100, and an annual management fee of 1 per cent. There is also a transaction charge of £15, plus commission on purchases of up to £7,000 of 1.4 per cent, less on larger amounts.

Investment managers Taylor Young provide a similar service, but without imposing an investment minimum. They charge an initial 1 per cent setting up charge plus an annual fee of 1 per cent. The commission charged on each transaction is 0.75 per cent.

Marlin Management have been running an investment trust advisory service since 1957. The minimum investment is normally £5,000 but they do accept as little as £1,500 provided investors are happy with just one or two investment trusts. There is an initial charge of 1 per cent, with a minimum of £50, and an administration fee of £50 a year. The commission charged on each transaction is £8 on a purchase, £12.80 on a sale. Unlike the other advisory services Marlin give themselves an incentive to do well for their clients by charging a performance fee of 5 per cent of any increase in the value of each portfolio.

Before NatWest Wood Mackenzie lost their private client department, they ran an investment trust management service. This is now operated by Edinburgh stockbrokers Robert White, who buy in NatWest Wood Mackenzie research. The minimum investment is £20,000. The initial fee is 5 per cent, and the annual fee is the greater of £300 or 0.3 per cent. There is commission of 1.65 per cent on each transaction.

Olliff & Partners are a new firm of stockbrokers who set up shop in June 1987 with the idea of carving out for themselves a sizeable slice of the investment trust market. Started by a former Warburg Securities man, they are mainly interested in big institutional clients.

However, they do operate a private client investment service, but only for the very wealthy. The minimum individual share purchase is £25,000, and the minimum portfolio is £100,000. The commission is low, just 0.75 per cent on the first £25,000, and 0.5 per cent above that.

OTHER WAYS OF BUYING SHARES

You can buy and sell shares through a solicitor, accountant, a bank manager, even some building societies. They in turn instruct a stockbroker to do the deal on your behalf. Obviously, this is not as good as talking to your own stockbroker directly, and there are inevitably going to be delays.

Most of the big clearing banks now own their own firms of stockbrokers. However, with the exception of Barclays with Barclayshare, bank customers are still required to channel their stock market business through their bank managers – they don't have direct access to the bank's stockbroker, and most clearing banks are charging relatively high minimum commissions. At Barclays, the minimum commission is £16 with an additional half-yearly charge of £10, Lloyds imposes a minimum charge of £20 with a handling fee of up to £5, Midland's minimum is £20 and National Westminster's £25.

Most stockbrokers deal for their clients over the telephone during working hours. 'Shareline' is a new telephone dealing service which is available daily from 10am. to 4pm., including Saturdays and Sundays. It is owned by British Telecom and Birmingham stockbrokers Albert E. Sharp, and the minimum commission is £15. You can contact the service on 021-200 2244.

A handful of building societies have also introduced 'no-frills' dealing services at some of their branches. Among the big building societies, Cheltenham & Gloucester, National & Provincial, Nationwide Anglia, and the Bristol & West all now offer this facility.

Avoid share dealers like the plague. Since Big Bang, stockbrokers can act as brokers (i.e. buying and selling shares to the public) as well as market makers (i.e. fixing the price at which shares change hands). But to avoid the obvious conflict of interest, the two functions have to be kept entirely separate.

Share dealers have no such scruples, and it isn't always clear which hat they are wearing when they recommend a share. It is not unusual to find share dealers plugging shares simply because they have them on their books and can't get rid of them. Beware also share dealers who offer no-commission dealing. It's an illusion. All the share dealer is doing is widening the spread between the price at which he buys and sells the shares.

Share shops, so long as they are run by stockbrokers rather than share dealers, are definitely worth investigating. You can deal there and then, and if you like the idea of sampling the Stock Exchange's own electronic gadgetry, this is the place to do it. Debenhams run three share shops: in their Oxford Street store, in Bristol and in the up-market Harvey Nichols in Knightsbridge. Minimum commission is £22. Birmingham brokers Smith Keen Cutler operate two share shops: one in the New Street, Birmingham, branch of Midland Bank, the other in the Wolverhampton branch of the West Bromwich Building Society. Their minimum commission is £20.

WHERE TO FIND THE STOCKBROKERS AND THE ADVISORY SERVICES

Top stockbrokers
Barclays de Zoete Wedd
2 Swan Lane
London EC4R 3TS
Tel: 01-623 2323

James Capel
James Capel House
PO Box 551
6 Bevis Marks
London EC3A 7JQ
Tel: 01-621 0011

NatWest Wood Mackenzie
(now part of County NatWest Securities)
Kintore House
74-77 Queen Street
Edinburgh EH2 4NS
Tel: 031-225 8525

Drapers Gardens
12 Throgmorton Avenue
London EC2P 2ES
Tel: 01-382 1000 or 01-638 6000

Warburg Securities
1 Finsbury Avenue
London EC2M 2PA
Tel: 01-606 1066

Investment trust advisory services
The Marlin Management Co
Harpley Green
Clifton-on-Terne
Worcester
WR6 6HG
Tel: 088 67435

Olliff & Partners
32 Threadneedle Street
London EC2R 8BA
Tel: 01-374 0191

Taylor Young Investment Management
45 Curlew Street
Butlers Wharf
London SE1 2ND
Tel: 01-407 3452

Touche Remnant Financial Management
Mermaid House
2 Puddle Dock
London EC4V 3AT
Tel: 01-236 8181

Robert White & Co
Kintore House
74-77 Queen Street
Edinburgh EH2 4NS
Tel: 031-243 4500

7 INVESTMENT TRUSTS COME IN ALL SHAPES AND SIZES

If there were such a thing as a typical investment trust, it would be large (e.g. more than £250 million), have a wide geographical spread of investments and aim to provide above average capital and income growth. Leading investment trusts such as *Alliance, British Investment Trust, Edinburgh Investment Trust, Foreign & Colonial, Globe, Scottish Mortgage, TR Industrial,* and *Witan* all fit this description.

This wide geographical spread of investments is a long-standing feature of investment trusts and one which they can justly claim to have pioneered. The investment trusts which emerged in the latter half of the last century gave small investors the chance to invest at least part of their savings overseas. And there was a time, not so long ago, when the big city institutions put their money in investment trusts rather than employ their own teams of overseas investment managers.

THE CASE FOR THE LARGE GENERAL INVESTMENT TRUST

There is a very good case to be made for the large trust with a spread of overseas investments. Once you are convinced that putting at least some of your money into equities is likely, over the long term, to be a good bet, you then have to decide how best to do it.

Most small investors don't have the time, energy, or expertise to invest in individual shares, beyond perhaps two or three privatisation issues. Apart from anything else, the risks of investing in just one or two shares are obviously greater than choosing a collective investment scheme, such as an investment trust, unit trust or insurance bond, where the risks are spread over a larger number of shares.

Small investors who want to invest overseas are even less likely to know which shares to buy, even if they knew how to do it. The advantage of large overseas investment trusts, or unit trusts for that matter, is that these decisions are made for you by experts. And not only should these experts be able to choose the right shares, they can take a view on how the various stock markets are going to perform and alter the balance of their portfolios accordingly. All they need to do is get their decisions right more often than wrong for the fund to perform better than average.

THE DEVELOPMENT OF SPECIALIST INVESTMENT TRUSTS

Specialist investment trusts with narrower investment objectives are by no means a new development. Many of the very earliest investment trusts started life as specialists. *Fleming Overseas,* for example, was incorporated in 1887 as the *British Steamship Investment Trust* and invested in ships and shipping companies. It became a general trust in the 1920s after British shipping went through a bad patch during and after the First World War. But the drive to specialise only developed into a craze in the early 1980s.

The impetus came from the marketing men. They watched how successful unit trusts were with their specialist unit trusts. They also argued that smaller city institutions still needed the overseas investment expertise of investment trusts. So why not give them investment trusts specialising in particular overseas markets? This gave rise to investment trusts specialising in Japan, the Far East, and the United States. There are even some overseas investment trusts which specialise twice over by investing only in smaller companies in their chosen area. With some notable exceptions investors have not done particularly well putting their money into specialist investment trusts.

It is relatively cheap to launch a new unit trust, and many get marketed just because their speciality happens to be flavour of the month. Investment trusts are more expensive to launch (they need to produce a full scale prospectus) which is why they can't be easily accused of launching new investment trusts just because a particular speciality is all the rage. Nonetheless, there are investment trusts which put their money into just one market sector such as energy, raw materials, plantations, technology, property and venture capital. And there are also a growing number of investment trusts which place their faith in smaller companies.

The AITC divides its 158 members into various categories to help potential investors track down the investment trust which suits them best.

There are 13 categories. Some contain as many as 27 trusts, others have as few as four or five. They are:

AITC category	number of trusts
Capital and income growth: general	24
Capital and income growth: UK	5
Capital growth: general	8
Capital growth: international	27
Capital growth: North America	6
Capital growth: Far East	10
Capital growth: Japan	9
Capital growth: commodities and energy	5
Capital growth: technology	4
Income growth	10
Smaller companies	17

Sector performance figures are given in the table at the end of this chapter.

Japanese and Far Eastern trusts

The Japanese and Far Eastern investment trusts have more than made up for the generally lacklustre performance of the specialists, even though following the crash of autumn 1987, they are now selling on historically wide discounts. The very earliest funds are now 16 years old, and their performance can only be described as phenomenal.

Investing through an investment trust or unit trust is the only practical way for private investors to participate in the extraordinary success of the Japanese economy and the growth which has spilled over into the whole Far Eastern region. When you invest in an overseas fund, you are effectively investing in that country's currency as well as its stock market. And investors in Japanese and Far Eastern investment trusts have benefited from the strength of the Yen as well as the strong performance of their investments.

The very first Japanese investment trust, *GT Japan*, was launched by GT in March 1972. If you had invested £1,000 at the beginning of 1978, ten years later your shares would have been worth £9,132, and assets per share would have increased from 33p to 311p.

GT have always had a very strong presence in the Far East. *GT Japan* started life being managed out of GT's Hong Kong office. But it wasn't long before they opened a research office in Tokyo. Around half the £3.6 billion which GT manages in unit trusts, investment trusts and on behalf of pension funds, is invested in the Far East.

It's a very different approach from Edinburgh Fund Managers, who started the second Japan investment trust *Crescent Japan* just a month after GT, and who have always managed their Far Eastern investments from their base in Edinburgh.

Crescent Japan and *GT Japan* have been friendly rivals since the beginning, and both have done almost equally well for their shareholders, as the performance figures in Appendix 1 show.

The number of Japanese and Far Eastern investment trusts increased dramatically during the drive for specialisation in the early and middle 1980s. New investment trusts were launched by Baillie Gifford and Martin Currie, while groups such as Fleming, Foreign & Colonial, Drayton and Touche Remnant took at least one of their existing investment trusts and transformed them into Japanese or Far Eastern investment trusts.

However, during the early months of 1988, the very wide discounts triggered off by the stockmarket crash brought two Japanese specialists into conflict with a number of their shareholders. *Drayton Japan* which only started specialising in the Japanese market in 1982, had proposals to turn itself into a split capital trust investing mainly in the UK. These proposals were rejected by the shareholders for want of a cash alternative. *Crescent Japan* defended its record as an investment trust in the face of demands to turn itself into a unit trust to eliminate the discount to net assets.

American trusts

Investment trusts are traditionally big North American investors. It is quite common for investment trusts to have at least a fifth of their portfolios invested in North America. Given the history, it is surprising that there are so few investment trusts which specialise in North America alone. But from the investor's point of view, it's no bad thing. The poor performance of North American equities and the relative weakness of the once mighty dollar are reflected in their performance.

Some of the North American investment trusts go back a very long way. Others, like the Japanese investment trusts, grew out of internal changes during the early 1980s. *Fleming American* and *TR North American* emerged out of other investment trusts in 1982. *Gartmore American* followed in 1984. But in April 1987, stockbrokers NatWest Wood Mackenzie worked out that shareholders in *Fleming American* and *TR North American* lost out following the shift in investment objectives. Only at *Gartmore American* was the change judged to be neutral.

Other sector specialists

The stock market can easily be divided up into its component parts, and fund managers love doing it. After all, an investment trust which only invests in one sector makes their job so much easier – they have far fewer shares to choose from. But judging from the performance of most of these sector specialists, it isn't a recipe for excellent returns. Almost all the energy, commodity and technology investment trusts have a very poor record.

Most private investors should give these sector specialists a wide berth unless they know the industry concerned inside out and are as confident as they can be that it is due for a re-rating.

Most investment trust investors are looking for long-term capital and possibly income growth. On past history, these sector specialists are unlikely to deliver it. But they can have occasional flashes of short-lived brilliance. For example, *Viking Resources* which set out to specialise in the North Sea, had assets per share of 29p in March 1976 and a share price of 15p. Five years later, assets per share had grown to 106p and the share price to 98p, levels which have hardly been seen since. Investors in *Viking* who sold out at the top as the world's oil shortage became an oil glut did very well. For those still stuck in there, it's been a struggle ever since, in spite of a change of investment policy in the summer of 1986. The main interest in the shares comes from the stakes being built up by Antipodean entrepreneurs, Ron Brierley and Alan Bond.

Technology specialist *Independent* also had its heyday.

Independent's niche is in electronics, and between June 1981 and June 1983, assets per share grew from 149p per share to 371p, and the share price more than doubled from 160p to 333p. Then the electronics boom fizzled out, and the shares have never returned to these levels.

With these sector specialists timing is all. Most private investors have a hard job best-guessing the direction of the market as a whole, let alone just one corner of it. And in reality these funds are designed for the institutions. Take the example of a pension fund manager who feels his pension fund ought to be invested 10 per cent in the electronics sector. Instead of buying the individual shares himself, he can buy a sector specialist like *Independent* instead.

Property trusts

For the private investor the one exception to this rule might be a property trust. *TR Property* has performed well since it emerged from Trust Union in 1982. Then there is the extraordinary *Trust of Property Shares*. This investment trust regularly appears top in the performance tables, and at one time during 1987 the shares actually stood at a near 80 per cent premium to net asset value. More a property company than an investment trust, at least half its portfolio is investing in Tops Estates, a successful quoted property company, controlled by the investment managers. *Value and Income* has not yet established a track record for the new policy which it has followed since 1986 of investing part of its portfolio in higher-yielding property.

However, it must be borne in mind that property is by no means a dead cert, as anyone who lived through the credit squeeze and ensuing property crash of the early 1970s will testify.

WHERE UNIT TRUSTS CANNOT TREAD

There are an increasing number of investment trusts specialising in venture capital and unlisted companies. It's a field which investment trusts and Business Expansion Scheme Funds have to themselves, with unit trusts effectively barred from such involvement, except in a very limited way.

It's not a new idea. *Electra* has been investing in unlisted companies since 1935. Its share performance has been slightly below average in recent years, but its asset performance is sound, and here at least there is absolutely no suggestion that investing in unlisted companies means an unacceptable level of risk.

But it's obviously a field where the investment managers need to know what they are doing. *F & C Enterprise,* launched in 1981, came unstuck when it lost money on company start-ups and US high-technology stocks. The fund has now changed its emphasis, with money now going to management buy-outs. Nonetheless, the shares, which stood at 19p at the end of 1981, languished at around 27p six years later. *London American Ventures,* formerly *London Trust,* is another of the walking wounded from this sector. It has written off

£7.5 million of £10 million it invested in Tony Palmer's film biography of Wagner. *London American Ventures* has now drawn a veil over this period, and made a fresh start as a US venture capital investment trust.

AITC CATEGORY PERFORMANCE

To 31.12.87 Base 100	Share price performance over:				Share price total return over:			
Sector	1 year	3 years	5 years	10 years	1 year	3 years	5 years	10 years
CAP & INCOME GROWTH: GENERAL	88.7	137.8	225.9	380.0	90.7	148.7	259.2	531.1
CAP & INCOME GROWTH: UK	109.8	167.9	271.3	419.0	113.5	187.4	332.5	679.5
CAP GROWTH: GENERAL	85.9	122.9	186.0	417.1	87.0	127.9	200.2	513.2
INTERNATIONAL	79.1	128.2	207.6	365.8	80.3	135.0	229.5	486.5
NORTH AMERICA	72.2	88.5	126.5	249.4	73.4	92.8	138.3	320.6
FAR EAST	82.2	134.3	243.6	451.5	82.8	138.9	260.2	584.1
JAPAN	101.0	147.3	310.1	665.5	101.2	148.9	318.5	820.0
COMMODITY/ENERGY	91.9	95.6	125.5	188.1	94.1	103.4	142.4	267.1
TECHNOLOGY	81.3	87.3	119.1	365.9	82.5	90.8	129.4	484.4
INCOME GROWTH	98.1	143.5	227.9	395.8	101.2	158.4	269.9	575.4
SMALLER COMPANIES	105.8	161.5	240.9	446.0	107.7	173.7	276.2	641.1
SPECIAL FEATURES	103.4	151.7	227.8	427.8	105.4	163.6	261.8	614.8
AVERAGE PERFORMANCE	90.1	133.5	213.7	389.3	91.8	142.7	241.8	538.1
SPLIT-LEVEL AVERAGE PERF	99.2	168.8	324.9	730.8	99.4	169.7	328.2	751.8

CONTD

To 31.12.87
Base 100

Sector	Net asset value performance over:				Net asset value total return over:			
	1 year	3 years	5 years	10 years	1 year	3 years	5 years	10 years
CAP & INCOME GROWTH: GENERAL	91.5	131.7	205.9	389.1	93.2	139.4	227.8	500.0
CAP & INCOME GROWTH: UK	109.9	162.2	252.1	404.6	113.0	177.4	295.4	596.7
CAP GROWTH: GENERAL	88.3	119.1	173.1	422.1	89.3	123.2	183.6	495.0
INTERNATIONAL	86.0	126.8	193.7	368.3	87.1	132.2	209.1	455.6
NORTH AMERICA	80.1	89.7	131.1	257.5	81.1	93.1	140.4	311.3
FAR EAST	89.3	153.2	259.8	474.6	89.8	157.3	273.9	574.8
JAPAN	104.1	169.6	354.2	680.3	104.2	170.8	362.0	794.2
COMMODITY/ENERGY	89.5	82.9	98.8	173.5	91.1	88.0	108.6	223.1
TECHNOLOGY	86.4	92.3	126.3	335.4	87.0	94.6	133.3	408.4
INCOME GROWTH	98.1	136.1	207.9	390.9	100.8	147.7	238.5	524.5
SMALLER COMPANIES	106.1	148.7	224.9	437.1	108.0	157.8	250.4	576.4
SPECIAL FEATURES	106.0	151.2	222.2	441.1	107.6	160.5	248.0	586.7
AVERAGE PERFORMANCE	93.6	131.3	202.4	393.2	95.0	138.2	222.3	502.4
SPLIT-LEVEL AVERAGE PERF	106.5	163.0	272.8	507.5	106.6	163.2	273.2	509.8

Source: AITC Statistics Service

8 MANY DIFFERENT WAYS OF INVESTING

There is more to investment trusts than their ordinary shares, and many people have no idea that there are other ways of putting money into investment trusts which might suit them as well as, if not better than, the conventional route. Investment trusts can offer this range of investments because their company structure gives them the freedom to raise money in a number of different ways.

EQUITY INVESTMENTS

With an equity investment, the shareholder becomes a part-owner of the company. Equity shareholders invest their money in the knowledge that their money is at risk. If the company goes bust, it is the equity shareholders who are paid out last, and in many cases of bankruptcy, shareholders end up getting nothing. However, their risk is limited to the extent of their investment – it is never greater.

Ordinary shares

Ordinary shares are the commonest equity investment. When people refer to equities, they are generally talking about the ordinary shares of companies. And when anyone talks about putting money into investment trusts, they are usually referring to the ordinary shares. It is the ordinary shares which everyone in the City spends so much time analysing, and to which net asset values, yields and discounts are all related.

Preference shares

There are other forms of equity investment. Some investment trusts issue preference shares. With preference shares the income on the shares is fixed when they are first issued. In most cases the income or yield is higher than the income paid on ordinary shares.

Many preference shares include the word 'cumulative' in their title. This tells you that if a dividend payment is missed, it will be paid at some time in the future or when the shares are repaid. As their name implies, preference shareholders take preference over ordinary shareholders when an investment trust is wound up or taken over. But in other respects the rights of preference shareholders are restricted, and they are not generally permitted to vote at annual general meetings.

Preference shares behave more like a fixed-interest stock than an ordinary share, and the price is influenced mainly by what happens to interest rates. If interest rates fall, the price of the preference shares rises, and if interest rates rise, the price falls.

Not many investment trusts have a fixed date on which they are to be wound up. When there is no winding up date, preference shares are an open-ended commitment, because you don't know when, if ever, you are going to be repaid, although you can of course buy and sell the preference shares on the stock market just like any other shares. The performance of these preference shares can be quite volatile, rather like those Government stocks with no fixed redemption date such as War Loan and Consols.

Few preference share prices are quoted in the newspapers and it is quite hard for the small investor to find out about them. They are mainly of interest to institutional shareholders, especially pension funds, who tend to be long-term holders of preference shares. With one or two exceptions, such as the new types of preference shares discussed later, private investors interested in a fixed interest stock are probably better off sticking with Government stocks or local authority bonds.

Warrants

Warrants give you the right to buy a company's shares at a fixed price some time in the future. They are effectively a traded option, except that they normally have much longer to run, and like traded options, they can be bought and sold on the stock market. Warrants have always occupied a very specialised corner of the investment world. In the 1960s and 1970s, a handful of property and secondary banking companies issued them. Today, blue chip companies such as Burton, Metal Box, P & O, Pilkington, Thorn, and United Biscuits all have warrants, but it's among investment trusts that the the biggest concentration of warrants is to be found.

No one should delude themselves about warrants. They are a high risk investment, because they offer investors an element of gearing, or what the Americans call 'leverage'. When markets are booming, warrants rise faster than the shares to which they are linked, but when markets go down, warrants fall faster.

To demonstrate how they work, let's take the very simplest example, a hypothetical investment trust, *Get Rich Quick,* whose ordinary shares stand at 100p. If *Get Rich*'s warrants give you the right to buy shares at 75p, then the warrants change hands for around 25p (100p less 75p.) If the price of *Get Rich* rises to 125p, then the warrants will double to 50p (125p less 75p). But by the same token, if the price of the ordinary shares falls to 75p, the warrants are worthless and you have lost your entire investment, at least until the market picks up.

Take an example from real life: *Throgmorton Trust* specialises in smaller companies. You can buy warrants which give you the right to buy shares in *Throgmorton* at 195p between now and 1993. On 16

September 1987, a month before the crash, *Throgmorton's* shares stood at 547p and the warrants were changing hands at 361p. A month after the crash, on 18 November the shares had fallen to 360p, a decline of 34 per cent, but the warrants had fallen much faster to 188p, a decline of 48 per cent.

Chapter 10 explains warrants in more detail.

Split capital shares

Split capital investment trusts have undergone a renaissance in the last couple of years – so much so that several managers have at least initially eliminated the discount on their existing trusts by converting them into split capital trusts.

Split capital trusts offer not just one class of ordinary share, but two and sometimes more. The shares may vary in their detail, but the basic pattern is the same. The capital shares get no dividend, but all the capital growth, while the income shares get all the dividends, but no capital growth. Split capital trusts have much to offer the private investor, and Chapter 9 takes a closer look at their attractions.

In the 1960s some investment trusts opted to issue 'B' shares rather than adopt the split capital structure. The intention was the same, and in many ways 'B' shares are similar to the capital shares of split capital investment trusts. The 'B' shareholder gets an annual scrip issue instead of a dividend. But a change in the tax treatment of 'B' dividends means that investors now pay income tax on their scrip issues. This rather defeats the purpose and most 'B' shares have now been converted into ordinary shares. In fact, 'B' shares are now not much more than a footnote in investment trust history.

BORROWINGS

Investment trusts have traditionally borrowed money through the stock market with issues of loan stocks and debenture stocks.

Debenture and loan stocks

These are fixed interest investments which work in the same way as Government stocks or local authority bonds. They also have much in common with preference shares, the main difference being that most loan and debenture stocks have a fixed date on which they are repaid, but most preference shares don't. And whereas preference shares are classified as part of a company's equity, loan and debenture stocks form part of a company's borrowings.

Your money is safer invested in loan and debenture stocks than in preference shares. In the event of a winding up, liquidation or bankruptcy, loan and debenture stock holders are repaid before preference shareholders who in turn are repaid before equity shareholders. Debenture stocks are the safest of all. These are secured on the assets of the company.

In practice though, small investors don't need to worry too much about the security of an investment trust's fixed interest stock. It is not impossible for an investment trust to go bust, but it hasn't happened since the very early days.

Convertible loan stocks

Convertible loan stocks are fixed interest loan stocks which carry the right to convert into ordinary shares on terms set out when the stock is issued. Convertibles, as they are usually called, are less volatile than the ordinary shares to which they are linked. Convertibles are the classical defensive investment, and in a stock market crash they won't fall as sharply as the ordinary shares. This is because the price of a convertible is supported by its yield, which is higher than the yield on the ordinary shares. But what you win on the roundabouts you lose on the swings, and in a stock market boom, convertibles don't rise as fast as the ordinary shares.

There are a number of investment trust convertibles. Take the example of *Shires*. This investment trust has an 11 per cent convertible unsecured loan stock which will be redeemed at par in March 2004. The stock carries the right to convert into the ordinary shares on the basis of one ordinary share for every £2 worth of stock on 31 March in any year between 1988 and 2003.

On 16 September 1988, a month before the stock market crash, *Shires'* ordinary shares stood at 250p, while the convertible stood at 129.25p. *Shires* entered the stock market crash with a high proportion of its portfolio invested in fixed interest securities, so the price of the ordinary shares held up remarkably well, and the convertibles even better. A month after the crash, on 19 November, *Shires'* ordinary shares had fallen to 208p, a fall of 17 per cent, while the convertible had fallen to 117.5p, a fall of just nine per cent.

NEW IDEAS

There has been a recent revival in the fortunes of the investment trust fixed interest market. A handful of imaginative managers are pioneering some interesting new ideas, often with the idea of eliminating the discount on their ordinary shares. There are debentures with an escalating rate of interest, preference shares where both the capital value and the dividends are increased, and zero-dividend preference shares where the dividend is rolled up in the capital value of the shares – ideal for higher rate taxpayers.

STUDS

It all began in 1982 with the stepped interest debenture stock developed by Scottish fund managers, Baillie Gifford. These stocks, which are now known as STUDS, start by paying a low rate of interest which is then increased year by year until it reaches a predetermined level.

STUDS were developed to get round the problem of the gap between what investment trusts earn on their investments and the interest they must pay on their borrowings. An investment trust which borrows money must invest it so that it produces enough income to cover the interest payments on the borrowings. If it can't, it must cut its dividend. STUDS ingeniously solve the problem by paying a low rate of interest to begin with. The managers then cross their fingers and hope the yield on their new investments rises sufficently to cover the year by year increases in interest payments.

However, STUDS have only limited appeal for private investors, and Baillie Gifford say that most of their investors are pension funds who are attracted by the growing yield. Nonetheless, investors nearing retirement and who are looking for a safe home for the lump sum from their firm's pension scheme might do worse than to look at STUDS if they want an escalating income.

Split capital structures

In May 1987, *River & Mercantile* decided to go for a split capital structure, but instead of opting for the traditional two classes of shares, (income and capital), they proposed a third entirely new category of share: a stepped preference share similar to STUDS except that in this case the capital as well as the dividend increases each year.

In September 1987, *Scottish National* went one step further with a similar proposal to convert into a split capital trust, but this time with four different classes of shares: income, capital, stepped preference and the first-ever zero dividend preference share.

A month later, *River Plate & General* went split level and combined it with an issue of zero dividend preference shares.

As we saw in the last chapter, many investment trusts are putting their faith in specialisation as the best way of attracting new investors. Investment trusts like *River & Mercantile, Scottish National* and *River Plate & General* are taking a different approach. They are using the flexibility of investment trusts to create new forms of investment which can be almost tailor made to suit any and every investment need. The risk-taker who wants capital growth can go for the capital shares of a split capital trust or warrants, while conservative higher rate taxpayers might like the look of a zero dividend preference share.

All these new investments vary in their detail. The structure of the available stepped preference shares and the zero dividend preference shares is given below. Split capital trusts are explained in the next chapter.

River & Mercantile Stepped Preference shares

Initial dividend in the year to end December 1987 is 4.2p net per share, 5.75 per cent gross. The dividend and capital value is increased by 5 per cent a year compound until 1999. The investment trust is to be wound up on 30 April 2000, by which time the dividend will have grown to 7.92p net, 9.1p gross per cent and the capital value, at which they are to be repaid, will be 188.6p a share. At 100p, their initial price, the gross redemption yield is 10.8 per cent. At the beginning of February 1988, the shares stood at 104p with a gross redemption yield of 10.3 per cent.

Scottish National Stepped Preference shares

The initial dividend in the year to end September 1988 is 5 per cent net, or 6.85 per cent gross. As at *River & Mercantile* the dividend and capital value is increased by 5 per cent a year, but in this case the investment trust is to be wound up slightly earlier at the end of September 1998, by which time the dividend will have increased to 8.144p net, 11.157 gross, and the capital value to 17lp, giving a gross redemption yield of 11.71 per cent at 100p. At the beginning of February 1988 the shares had risen to 110.5p, giving a gross redemption yield of 10.86%.

Scottish National Zero Dividend Preference shares

These shares receive no income at all, but the shares which were initially worth 100p are to be repaid at 325p when the investment trust is wound up at the end of September 1998. This gives an income tax-free redemption yield of 11 per cent. At the beginning of February 1988, the shares had risen to 102.5p, giving a gross redemption yield of 11.11 per cent.

River Plate & General Zero Dividend Preference shares

Like the *Scottish National* zero dividend preference shares, these preference shares receive no income. They were issued at 35 1/4p and are to be repaid at 100p at the end of October 1996. This gives a tax free redemption yield of 11.85 per cent. By the beginning of February 1988 the shares had risen to 39.75p and had a gross redemption yield of 10.51 per cent.

9 SPLIT CAPITAL INVESTMENT TRUSTS

Split capital investment trusts have been around since the 1960s. The very first, *Dualvest,* was wound up in February 1987. They were invented at a time when investment trusts were starting to lose their popularity with investors, and it was thought that one way of keeping them happy was to give them a variety of shares to choose from.

Most split capital investment trusts have a fixed life and the date on which they are to be wound up is set out in advance in the prospectus. The performance of an investment trust is made up of two elements: the growth or otherwise in the capital value of the underlying investments; and the income it gets from those investments. With most investment trusts, the shareholders share these two elements equally.

TWO CLASSES OF SHARES

Split capital investment trusts are different. Here there are traditionally two classes of shares. In most cases the capital shares are entitled to all the capital growth, but don't get a dividend. This makes them attractive to higher-rate taxpayers. The income shares receive all the income, but the shareholders are normally entitled only to get back the par value – usually the same as the issue price – of the shares on winding up.

Split capital investment trusts are effectively a way of introducing an element of gearing without having to borrow the money to do it. For example, an investment trust with assets of £10 million might be financed by ordinary shares of £5 million and a capital reserve of £5 million. If those assets grew to £15 million, the shares see a 50 per cent increase in their net asset value.

If that same investment trust had a split capital structure, it might be financed by £2.5 million of capital shares and £2.5 million of income shares. With net assets of £10 million the capital shares have a net asset value of £7.5 million, financed by £2.5 million of shares, and all the capital reserve of £5 million. If net assets then grew to £15 million, the net asset value of the capital shares rises to £12.5

million – a rise of 66 per cent. An additional element of gearing or leverage is often introduced by issuing a greater number of income shares than capital shares.

THE DISADVANTAGES

It sounds fine in theory, but the structure of the early split capital investment trusts has proved to be less than ideal in practice.

The capital shares have a tendency to fall in their early years and trade on very high discounts to their net asset values. This progressively narrows the nearer the investment trust is to its winding up date. Over the long term, however, the capital shares of split capital investment trusts have been outstandingly successful, with many right at the top of the performance tables.

The income shares have turned out to be less attractive. In the early years the price of the shares tends to rise above their net asset values as the stream of dividend income increases. The shares then fall back again as the winding up date approaches and the prospect of being repaid at their initial subscription price or par reasserts itself. As the table overleaf shows, this can throw up some very high running yields.

Income shares are not entirely without their uses. After all, you don't have to hold the shares until they are repaid, and if interest rates fall at a time when the stock market is stagnant, income shares can do very well. But more importantly, they have defensive qualities. In falling markets income shares fall less sharply than investment trust shares as a whole and much less sharply than their capital share counterparts.

Take the example of *Fundinvest*. On 15 September 1987, a month before the crash of 19 October, *Fundinvest*'s capital shares stood at 624p, and the income shares at 46p. On 18 November, a month after the crash, the capital shares had fallen to 460p, a drop of 26 per cent, while the income shares had shed just 2p to 44p, a fall of just 4 per cent. They can also be useful if you want a high yield while establishing a capital loss which you can offset against a claim for capital gains tax. The table below shows the running and redemption yields on the available income shares. To get round some of the problems associated with the traditional split capital structure, some investment trusts give their income shareholders a limited entitlement to capital growth, in return for which the capital shareholders get a small income.

Income shares

Investment trust	price	redemp- tion price	running yield	gross redemp- tion yield	term to wind-up
	p	p	%	%	yrs
Ambrose	70	52	24.29	16.49	3.12
Archimides	160	25	11.13	15.50	15.62
City & Commercial	45	25	16.18	15.26	4.97
Danae	82	52	10.10	4.57	14.88
Derby	150xd	25	9.91	13.54	15.88
English National Pref	255	–	5.72	–	–
English National Defd	185	–	4.27	–	–
Equity Consort Ord	410	–	4.82	–	–
Equity Consort Defd	680	–	4.04	–	–
Fulcrum	67	42	12.88	13.10	6.88
Fundinvest	46	25	25.52	16.85	2.63
Jove	91	51	9.01	11.82	11.88
M & G Dual	375	100	13.81	13.58	8.88
M & G Second Dual	165	50	12.50	13.49	9.80
New Throgmorton	96	30	6.92	11.73	20.63
Rights & Issues	75	60	7.95	–	–
River & Mercantile	98	100	7.93	11.82	12.21
River & Mercantile Geared	110	105.8	6.85	10.04	11.63
River Plate	91	100	9.56	14.40	8.70
St David's	108	100	9.00	11.31	6.40
SPLIT	265	100	13.34	14.67	8.88
SPRAIT	149	104	7.40	–	22.88
Scottish National	89	100	9.62	14.88	10.64
Throgmorton Dual	96	65	7.14	9.09	11.47
Tor	293	129	8.17	10.98	13.47
Triplevest	85	50	22.38	17.72	3.04
Yeoman	121	103	10.47	11.65	4.88

(1) Average price March 1987-March 1988
(2) Calculation of gross redemption yield assumes 7 per cent growth of portfolio

Source: Klienwort Grieveson Securities

RIVER AND MERCANTILE PAVE THE WAY

In the last couple of years a number of investment trust managers have used the split capital structure as a way of eliminating the discount on net assets. As a result, opting for a split capital structure is now considered one of the best alternatives to unitisation – the practice of turning an investment trust into a unit trust.

It all began with *River & Mercantile Geared Capital and Income Trust*. This investment trust introduced a number of pioneering new concepts which shed new light on the possibilities offered by the split capital structure. *River & Mercantile Geared Capital and Income Trust* was a new investment trust rather than a transformation of an existing one. It was offered for sale in the spring of 1986, and has a relatively short life – it is to be wound up in 1999. To avoid the problems normally associated with new split capital investment trusts, the capital shares were issued at a 50 percent discount to net asset value, while the income shares were issued at 50 per cent above their net asset value, but with the promise of a share in the capital growth of the portfolio.

It wasn't until the following year that *River & Mercantile* became the first existing investment trust to turn itself into a split capital trust using the ideas pioneered by its stable mate, *River & Mercantile Geared*. But instead of issuing only the two usual classes of shares, capital and income, it added two more: stepped preference shares and warrants. The aim was to narrow the overall discount on net asset value – it stood at around 12 per cent – by giving shareholders the same mix of capital and income as before, but in the form of several different classes of shares instead of just one.

Before they were issued in June 1987, it was assumed that the capital, income and stepped preference shares would all change hands for around 100p. At that price the capital shares were standing at a 55 per cent discount to net assets, and the income shares at a 60 per cent premium to net assets. On winding up in 2000, the stepped preference shares are to get 188.6p a share, the income shares 100p, and the capital shares are to get what's left. In a bull market the capital shares look like a good bet – a five per cent growth in net assets each year produces a gross redemption yield of 10.4 per cent, and with a growth rate of 7.5 per cent, the redemption yield rises to 15.2 per cent. A bear market shows what a risky strategy this can be. If the market can't produce this level of growth, what will be left for the capital shareholders once all the preference and income shareholders have been repaid?

These questions were reflected in *River & Mercantile*'s share prices following the market crash of October 1987. On 15 September 1987 the capital shares stood at 115p. A month after the crash on 18 November, they had fallen to 58p, a decline of 50 per cent. The income shares showed their defensive qualities with a fall from 100p to 87p, a decline of 13 per cent, while the stepped preference shares responding to a fall in interest rates actually rose from 93p to 102p, a rise of nearly 10 per cent.

OTHER SPLIT CAPITAL TRUSTS

Two other split capital transformations followed in the wake of *River & Mercantile*. With net assets of around £250 million, *Scottish National* is by far the largest to date. *Scottish National* followed the pattern established by *River & Mercantile*, but with one important refinement – they introduced an additional class of share, zero dividend preference shares, which are entitled to capital growth, but no income. This was done to relieve the investment managers of the need to produce a large income to service the dividend needs of the income and preference shareholders. *River Plate & General* was the next to take the split capital route. In addition to new income and capital shares, it also launched a new zero dividend preference share, and there was an issue of warrants as well.

Although there is no attempt to split income from capital, which is the basic feature of a split capital trust, Ivory & Sime's reconstruction of *Edinburgh American Assets* gave shareholders the chance to switch into a new investment trust, with two classes of shares. Called *Selective Assets*, 40 per cent of the shares come in the form of an Index loan stock where the capital and income performance is tied to the FT-Actuaries All Share Index. The remaining 60 per cent of the shares get what's left after the Index stockholders have been paid. If the trust's investments perform better than the Index, the shares will outshine the Index stock, but if the investments fail to match the Index, the Index stock will do better.

There is a snag in all this. Historically, few investment managers have managed consistently to beat the Index over a long period, so the Index stock looks a good bet, and it's hard to see anyone wanting the ordinary shares.

10 UNDERSTANDING WARRANTS

As investment trusts are becoming better known, private investors are often surprised to learn how many different ways there are of investing in them. Higher-rate taxpayers in particular stumble across investment trust warrants and wonder how they could have remained in such ignorance of their possible uses.

As we saw in Chapter 8, warrants are like a traded option. They give you the right to buy shares at some time in the future at a price fixed when the warrants were first issued. They don't pay a dividend. Unlike traded options, which have a maximum life of nine months, warrants normally have longer to run.

Warrants are a geared investment, which means the price rises faster than the ordinary shares when markets are rising, but falls faster when markets are in retreat. Warrants offer the prospect of good long-term growth with no income, which is why they are particularly suitable for higher-rate taxpayers.

There are around 50 investment trust warrants to choose from, and as you can see from the table at the end of the chapter they are all different.

HOW TO ASSESS THEM

If you are thinking of putting money into warrants you need to know how to assess them. The first thing to find out is how long the warrant has to run before the option to buy the underlying shares expires. The longer the better. If you don't mind locking your money away for a number of years, obviously the longer the warrant has to run, the more likely it is to show a profit.

The gearing ratio

The amount of gearing varies too. The higher the gearing, the greater the risk, but also the greater the potential reward. Gearing is measured by dividing the price of the ordinary shares by the price of the warrant. So if the share price stands at 100p and the warrants stand at 50p, the gearing ratio is 2:1. But if the warrant stands at 75p, the gearing ratio is 1.3:1.

Using this example it is easy to see how the warrant with the gearing ratio of 2 is the riskier of the two, but also offers the greater potential reward. If the investment trust ordinary shares rise by 20p to 120p, the 50p warrants might rise 20p to 70p, an increase of 40 per cent. The 70p warrants might also rise by 20p to 90p, an increase of 29 per cent. On the other hand if the investment trust ordinary shares fell 20p to 80p, the 50p warrants would fall further in percentage terms than the 70p warrant.

Of course, in real life nothing is quite so simple, and the relationship between the price of the warrant and the underlying share is never as neat as this. In fact, the price of warrants also depends on supply and demand, and the value the market puts on the amount of time left before the warrant expires.

Warrant premiums and discounts

The warrant premium is a measure of their value for money. At its simplest, warrants standing on a high premium are said to be expensive, and those on a low premium or discount are said to be cheap. The warrant premium compares the cost of buying the ordinary shares via the warrants with the cost of buying the shares directly.

To work out the cost of buying the ordinary shares via the warrants, you take the price of the warrant and add to it the price at which you can exercise your option to buy the ordinary shares. The percentage difference between this total and the share price is the premium. For example, the total for a warrant standing at 50p, with an exercise price of 75p, is 125p. If the ordinary shares are 100p, it is 25p more expensive to buy the shares via their warrants, which therefore means a premium of 25 per cent.

The premium on warrants gradually disappears as the warrant approaches the final date on which the option to buy the ordinary shares can be exercised. When you buy warrants it is important to remember that the proportion of the warrant price represented by the premium is effectively being eroded by time. In practice this may not matter. Many people who invest in warrants choose to sell them rather than exercise their right to buy the ordinary shares, in which case it's a good idea to buy warrants when the premium is low and sell them when it is high. Even if you are buying warrants in order to exercise them and buy the underlying shares, the ordinary shares will hopefully have risen sufficiently by the final date for the investment still to look a very good deal.

Very occasionally, you find investment trust warrants standing at a discount. In these circumstances, if dealing expenses don't erode the benefit, ordinary shareholders are better off selling their shares and buying the warrants.

In-the-money, out-of-the money

The price at which you can exercise most warrants is usually lower than the price of the underlying ordinary shares. These warrants are known as 'in-the-money'.

However, where the exercise price is above the underlying share price, the warrants are referred to as 'out-of-the-money'. In these cases, the warrants have no intrinsic value, and the price, which is usually only a few pence, represents time or hope value only. Take the example of *Gartmore Information.*The warrants carry the right to buy the ordinary shares at 64p before 1994. At the beginning of February 1988, the ordinary shares were quoted at just 47p. The warrants were 11p, which is the price investors were prepared to pay in the hope that the price of *Gartmore Information* would exceed 75p (exercise price plus warrant) before 1994.

Takeovers

A word of warning: anyone thinking of buying warrants (or convertible loan stocks for that matter) should realise that they could lose out if their investment trust is taken over. Warrantholders have no automatic right to be compensated for the loss of any time value remaining on their warrants. In most takeovers or reconstructions, the warrantholders are requested to exercise their option to buy the shares, and they are then treated just like any other ordinary shareholders.

The AITC has lobbied the Takeover Panel on behalf of warrantholders, but so far no one can agree a formula for compensating warrantholders for the loss of time value.

Buying and selling

Warrants are a tiny specialist market. If they have a major disadvantage, it is that they can be difficult to buy and sell, and even if you can get someone to quote you a price, the spread between the buying and selling price can be ludicrously wide.

Stockbrokers Warburg Securities who compiled the list of warrants below, also rate them for their marketability on a scale from 0 to 5, with 0 representing the virtually unsaleable, and 5 indicating a fairly active market.

Roger Adams and John Korwin-Szymanowski at Warburg Securities have compiled a list of golden rules for warrant investors, as follows:

- Go for warrants on a low premium. The lower the premium, the lower the risk.

- Go for in-the-money warrants with high gearing. These warrants give you the maximum exposure for the minimum investment, possibly freeing money for a less risky investment. One idea for nervous higher-rate taxpayers is to invest in a combination of risky highly geared warrants and the much safer zero-dividend preference shares pioneered by *Scottish National* and *River Plate & General.* Such a combination pays no income, so there is no income tax to pay, although there may be capital gains tax to pay when you sell.

- Go for warrants with a long life – at least four years is the suggested minimum.

- Avoid warrants linked to high income investment trusts. High income investment trusts tend to sacrifice capital for income growth, and a poor capital peformance from the ordinary shares affects the performance of the warrants.

- Don't forget that, by and large, the warrants which do best are those linked to the best performing investment trusts. So choose your warrants as if you were thinking of buying the ordinary shares.

- Make sure that your choice of warrant is easy to buy and sell and that there is normally a ready market for it.

INVESTMENT TRUST WARRANTS

At 1.2.88

Company	Subscription terms	Warrant price (p)	Ordinary price (p)	Gearing ratio	Warrant premium	Marketability
ATLANTIC ASSETS	1 ordinary at 80p anytime to 30th June 1997	10	43	4.3	109	4
AUSTRALIA INVESTMENT	1 ordinary at 93p 31st December 1988-92	18	78	4.3	42	1
AUSTRALIA INVESTMENT 'A'	1 ordinary at 143p 31st December 1988-93	12	78	6.5	99	1
BAILLIE GIFFORD JAPAN	1 ordinary at 100p 30th November 1988-89	322	420	1.3	0	2
BAILLIE GIFFORD SHIN NIPPON	1 ordinary at 50p 30th April 1988-96	29	71	2.4	11	2
BAILLIE GIFFORD TECHNOLOGY	1 ordinary at 100p 31st May 1988-95	15	75	5.0	53	2
CHILD HEALTH	1 ordinary at 71p 30th April 1988-92	15	37	2.5	132	1
CHILDREN'S MEDICAL	1 ordinary at 100p 30 days following Accounts 1988-92	20	95	4.8	26	1
CHINA & EASTERN	1 ordinary at 1 US dollar anytime between 1st October 1988 and 30th September 1991	40	75	1.9	29	2
CONSOLIDATED VENTURE SERIES '100'	1 ordinary at 100p 30 days following Accounts 1988-90 (March)	100	190	1.9	5	2

CONSOLIDATED VENTURE SERIES '120'	1 ordinary at 120p 30 days following Accounts 1987-93 (March)	90	190	2.1	11	2
CLYDESDALE	1 ordinary at 100p 31st December 1988-95	23	90	3.9	59	1
CONTINENTAL ASSETS	1 ordinary at 100p 30th April 1988-96	29	64	2.2	102	2
DANAE INVESTMENT	1 income and 1 capital for a total of 65p on 31st March and 30th September in any year	41	Inc 78 Cap 29	2.6	(1)	1
DERBY TRUST	1 capital at 115p 31st March and 30th September 1988-91	98	200	2.0	7	2
DRAYTON FAR EASTERN	1 ordinary at 101p 30th April 1988-91	118	221	1.9	(1)	2
EDINBURGH INVESTMENT	1 ordinary at 111p 31st July 1988-90	52	147	2.8	11	5
EFM DRAGON	1 ordinary at 10p 31st January 1989-96	4	7	1.8	100	2
ENGLISH & INTERNATIONAL	2 ordinary at 140p each 5th August 1988-93	163	200	2.5	11	2
F&C ENTERPRISE	1 ordinary at 20p 30th April 1988-91	16	27	1.7	33	1
F&C ENTERPRISE SERIES 'B'	1 ordinary at 31p 30th April 1988-91	11	27	2.5	56	1
F&C PACIFIC	1 ordinary at 77.5p 30th June 1988-94	40	112	2.8	5	3
FIRST SPANISH	1 ordinary at 100p 31st August 1988-97	22	60	2.7	103	3
FLEDGELING JAPAN	1 ordinary at US$1 or 70p at any time to 30th June 1990	26	73	2.8	14	2
GT VENTURE	1 ordinary at 100p 1st November 1988-93	21	75	3.6	61	1
GARTMORE EUROPEAN	1 ordinary at 354p 1st October 1988-96	100	260	2.6	75	2
GARTMORE INFORMATION	1 ordinary at 64p 1st April 1988-94	11	47	4.3	60	2

At 1.2.88

Company	Subscription terms	Warrant price (p)	Ordinary price (p)	Gearing ratio	Warrant premium	Marketability
GERMAN SECURITIES	1 ordinary at 100p 31st January 1988-90	25	91	3.6	37	1
GERMAN SMALLER COMPANIES	1 ordinary at 100p 31st August 1988-95	46	91	2.0	60	1
GREENFRIAR	1 ordinary at 112p 1st April 1988	215	314	1.5	4	1
HAMBROS	1 ordinary at 177p 31st July 1988-94	58	194	3.3	21	4
INDEPENDENT INVESTMENT	1 ordinary at 79p anytime to 30th June 1997	11	38	3.5	137	3
INVESTING IN SUCCESS	1 ordinary at 212p anytime to 30th April 1992	32	138	4.3	77	1
JAPAN ASSETS	1 ordinary at 64p 31st January 1989-94	12	71	5.9	7	3
LONDON AMERICAN VENTURE	1 ordinary at 110p 31st July 1990 1 ordinary at 125p 31st July 1995 1 ordinary at 140p 31st July 2000	20	47	2.4	180	2
MARTIN CURRIE PACIFIC	1 ordinary at 100p 30th June 1988-93	61	151	2.5	7	2
MELVILLE STREET	1 ordinary at 146p 31st August 1989-94	38	103	2.7	79	1
MOORGATE	1 ordinary at 257p 31st August 1988-97	40	203	5.1	46	1
MULTITRUST	1 ordinary at 60p 1st April 1989-1991	20	53	2.7	51	1
MURRAY VENTURES	1 ordinary at 165p 30th November 1988-89	88	246	2.8	3	2

NEW DARIEN	1 ordinary at 100p 31st July 1988	6	59	9.8	80	2
NEW THROGMORTON	1 capital at 50p anytime prior to 30th September 1993	63	101	1.6	12	3
NEW TOKYO	1 ordinary at 50p 30th June 1988	83	136	1.6	(2)	2
NEW TOKYO 'A'	1 ordinary at 159p 30th June 1989-98	Dealings 22nd February				2
OVERSEAS	1 ordinary at 202p 31st December 1988-98	Dealings 22nd February				2
PACIFIC ASSETS	1 ordinary at 100p 31st May 1988-95	51	106	2.1	42	2
PLANTATION TRUST	1 ordinary at 100p 31st August 1988-95	28	88	3.1	45	1
RENAISSANCE HOLDINGS	1 ordinary at 100p 30th June 1988-97	25	80	3.2	56	1
RIVER & MERCANTILE	1 capital at 300p anytime to 30th April 2000	24	58	2.4	459	3
RIVER PLATE	1 capital at 250p anytime to 31st October 1996	16	58	3.6	359	2
SAVE & PROSPER RETURN OF ASSETS	1 ordinary and 1 preferred for a total of 200p 1st June 1990-95	105	Pfd 149 Ord 135	2.7	7	2
SCOTTISH INVESTMENT	1 ordinary at 484p anytime up to 15th February 1995	68	354	5.2	58	5
SCOTTISH NATIONAL	1 capital at 300p anytime to 30th September 1998	13	48	3.7	552	3
SHIRES	1 ordinary at 182p 1st October 1988-93	40	218	5.5	2	2
STRATA	1 ordinary at 100p 31st January 1988-93	30	97	3.2	34	1
THROGMORTON TRUST	1 ordinary at 195p 30 days after AGM 1988-93	240	421	1.8	3	4
THROGMORTON USM	1 ordinary at 100p 28 days after AGM 1988-93	50	120	2.4	25	2

At 1.2.88

Company	Subscription terms	Warrant price (p)	Ordinary price (p)	Gearing ratio	Warrant premium	Marketability
VALUE AND INCOME	1 ordinary at 35.54p 1st July and 31st December 1988	19	51	2.7	7	2
VALUE AND INCOME '94'	1 ordinary at 70p 30th June, 31st December 1989/94	15	51	3.4	67	2
VANTAGE SECURITIES	1 ordinary at 57p 31st March 1988-92	90	125	1.4	18	1
WITAN	1 ordinary at 76.5p 1st August 1988-93	53	108	2.0	20	5

Source: Warburg Securities

11 FINDING THE RIGHT TRUST FOR YOUR REQUIREMENTS

The big attraction of investment trusts is their versatility – there is something for everyone. There are many different ways to put your money into investment trusts, some relatively unknown, most deserving a much better following, almost all offering better value for money than unit trusts or anything the high pressure insurance salesman can offer.

But before you finally make up your mind that an investment trust is for you, one word of warning. Whichever way you end up putting your money in investment trusts, remember you are making a long-term commitment. Don't invest any money that you think you might need back in less than five years. Investing in an investment trust is not like putting your money in a building society. There is never any guarantee that you can get back the full value of your investment just when you want it. When you put your money into investment trusts you are subject to the ups and downs of the stock market and possibly interest rates as well.

CLARIFY YOUR INVESTMENT AIMS

Take a close look at your financial circumstances. If you have money to invest what do you want that money to achieve for you?

For example, if you are working and have more than enough money to pay for life's little luxuries, you aren't interested in boosting your income: you want an investment which gives a high capital return. If you are retired, your needs are entirely different. You may need to boost your income, and you may want that income to grow.

Look at your tax position too. If you pay higher-rate tax you want to shield your investments from income tax. And if you face a capital gains tax bill some time in the future, you may want to establish a capital loss. All this is possible with investment trusts.

Know your financial self

No investment is worth sleepless nights. Wherever you invest, it is important that you should feel confident and comfortable with your choice. Never let anyone talk you into investing in something which is going to cause you endless anxiety. Make an effort to understand your attitude to money and what makes you tick when it comes to investing it.

The psychology of investment is fascinating. What makes some people keen to take a risk, while others quake in their boots each time their bank account goes into the red by a couple of pounds? The answer probably lies deeply buried in the psyche. But don't let that stop you from trying to place yourself somewhere on that line between the high-risk taker and the financial conservative.

Of course, your attitude to investment is at least partly determined by your circumstances. The wealthy, experienced stock market investor is much more likely to be prepared to take a risk than the novice only newly aware of the stock market and its potential.

The following examples illustrate how investment trusts can be used to suit almost anyone's investment needs.

THE HIGHER-RATE TAXPAYER WHO WANTS CAPITAL GROWTH, NO INCOME AND DOESN'T MIND TAKING A RISK

This investor should look at the capital shares of split capital trusts or warrants. Both investments are highly volatile – they tumble in falling markets and race ahead in rising markets. Capital shares benefit from the investment trust's capital growth. Warrants give you the right to buy shares at some time in the future at a predetermined price. Neither pays an income, which is handy if you pay higher-rate income tax and don't want to pay any extra tax.

THE HIGHER-RATE TAXPAYER WHO IS NORMALLY HAPPIER LEAVING MONEY ON DEPOSIT

This investor should make a beeline for one of the new zero-dividend preference shares offered by, for example, *Scottish National, River Plate & General* and *TR Technology.** With zero dividend preference shares, there is no dividend. Instead, the capital value of the shares rises by a set amount each year. The price and date on which the shares are repaid are determined in advance. There is, however, an element of risk. Unless you intend keeping the shares until they are repaid, your investment isn't entirely safe. The capital value can be affected by what happens to interest rates in the world outside.

Building societies and bank deposit accounts offer a poor after-tax return to higher-rate taxpayers. With zero- dividend preference shares there is no income tax to pay, so the higher-rate taxpayer can expect a much better return. But you may have to pay capital gains tax if your profit when you sell exceeds your annual capital gains tax exemption (£5,000 in the 1988-89 tax year). Zero-dividend preference shares are a new and innovative development. They are the ideal investment for higher-rate taxpayers.

---

*At the date of going to press only these trusts offered zero dividend preference shares.

THE INVESTOR WHO WANTS TO BOOST HIS INCOME

There are an almost endless number of places to invest a lump sum if you are in search of an income. It's a problem which faces anyone who inherits money, or who opts to take a lump sum from their firm's pension scheme when they retire.

Putting the money into a high-yielding investment trust is one of the best solutions so long as you don't need to maximise your income immediately. Your initial yield won't be the best available, but in the long-term you are likely to do better. This is because investment trusts aim to produce a steadily growing stream of dividend income. With most other forms of fixed interest investment your income is agreed at the outset, or fluctuates with interest rates.

And if you keep your money invested for at least five years, the capital value of your investment is likely to rise too. Most other lump sum investments only give back your original investment. Choose a trust which gives priority to income growth and has a good record of delivering it.

If, on the other hand, you do need a reasonable income right from the start, look at the new-style income shares issued by the latest split-level investment trusts including *General Consolidated, Grahams Rintoul, River & Mercantile America, River Plate & General, St. David's, Scottish National* and *Yeoman**. For example at the beginning of 1988 *Scottish National*'s income shares stood at around 87p which gave an after-tax yield of 7.2 per cent. The shares are repaid in 1998 at 100p. In the meantime the shares get the benefit of most of the income generated by *Scottish National*'s investments.

A COUPLE SAVING FOR SCHOOL FEES

An investment trust savings scheme is an excellent and cheap way of saving a regular amount each month. The accumulated fund can then be used to pay school fees as and when they are needed. Choose a general fund, and if you are a higher-rate taxpayer, find one with a lowish yield. If you don't want to spend the income, find a scheme where the dividends can be automatically reinvested. This won't save you any tax, it just means the dividend income becomes part of the accumulated fund.

Investment trust saving schemes are extremely flexible, and there is nothing to stop you investing additional lump sums if you suddenly find yourself with a bit of spare cash. Unit trust savings schemes are often recommended for school fees planning. But you are likely to do as well, if not better, if you choose an investment trust.

---

*At the date of going to press, these are the split-level investment trusts currently offering new-style income shares.

THE INVESTOR WHO LIKES THE IDEA OF INVESTING ON THE STOCK MARKET BUT DOESN'T KNOW WHICH SHARES TO BUY

Many investors have cut their stock market teeth on the Government's privatisation issues, and now want to go on to buy shares of their own choice, but don't know how. These investors should look no further than investment trusts. Choosing individual shares for yourself may be fun, but don't kid yourself that this is the best way of making money. With investment trusts you get a spread of investments and professional management.

THE INVESTOR WHO WANTS TO INVEST OVERSEAS

If you have built up a sizeable portfolio of UK shares, you may want to spread your risk further and invest some of your money overseas. With the world's capital markets becoming ever more international, it is becoming very easy for big institutional investors to invest in individual overseas companies. For private investors, that day is still some way off. Even if you knew which overseas companies you wanted to invest in, the cost of dealing in small amounts would rule it out. Your best bet is to invest through a collective investment scheme, either a unit trust or an investment trust. The majority of investment trusts have an overseas component, and they have traditionally held a high proportion of their investments in the United States. Even today most general investment trusts have at least a fifth of their funds invested in North America. But if you are interested in a particular market, there are also specialist investment trusts. The Japanese and Far Eastern investment trusts have an excellent record. There are also specialist North American, Australian, and European investment trusts. There are even two investment trusts which specialise in Germany, another in Spain, and one in Scandinavia.

THE INVESTOR FACED WITH A BIG CAPITAL GAINS TAX BILL

If you know you are likely to face a big capital gains tax bill in the next couple of years you can offset your liability and establish a capital loss by investing in one of the high yielding income shares which are standing at a premium to net assets, preferably one which is due to be wound up sometime over the next couple of years; during this time the shares must drop sharply as they fall to the level at which they are to be repaid. The compensation is the high running yield, and as such this is not an option which makes much sense for higher-rate taxpayers.

12 INVESTMENT TRUST PERFORMANCE

Looking at performance is one way of judging investment trusts. It can't tell us everything, but it's a useful place to start. Of course, there is never any guarantee that an investment trust which has done well in the past is going to continue to do so in the future.

Nonetheless, taken with a dose of scepticism and a modicum of understanding, the performance tables are an indispensable guide through the investment trust maze. They can lead us to the investment management groups with the best overall record across a range of trusts; they can show us which investment trusts have increased their dividends the fastest; and over the short term they can illustrate which sectors are performing the best.

MEASURING PERFORMANCE

There are three principal ways of looking at investment trust performance, each one shedding a slightly different light on the matter.

If you want to know if the investment managers are doing a good job look at *net asset* performance. This tells you what is happening to the capital value of the underlying investments, i.e. whether they are growing or not.

But they won't necessarily tell you how well or badly the shares themselves have done. For this you must look for the *share price* performance. This will be different from net asset performance because investment trust share prices rarely mirror their net asset value, and as we have already seen, most investment trusts stand at a discount to their net asset value.

Look at net asset and share price performance together and you get an idea of how an investment trust made its money. Did the investment managers do a good job? Or were they lucky in benefiting from the narrowing of the discount? Or was it a combination of the two?

It's easy to forget that there's more to investment trusts than just their capital performance. Don't overlook the fact that they also produce an income in the form of dividends. A good investment trust aims to produce a steadily increasing flow of dividends.

So if you want to know which trusts produced the best overall return look for the figures for *total return*. These are available in two forms: *net asset value total return* measures asset performance after reinvesting after-tax dividends; *share price total return* does the same, using the share price as the measure of performance.

Take the example of *Greenfriar* and *Lowland*, two investment trusts both from the Henderson stable, and both very successful. *Greenfriar* aims for capital growth, while *Lowland* puts the emphasis on income growth. Over the last ten years, to the end of December 1987, *Greenfriar* managed to increase net assets to give a total net asset return of £708 for every £100 invested. *Lowland* did even better with a total net asset return of £1,041 for every £100 invested. But the percentage of total return attributable to dividend income differed widely. With *Greenfriar* only 8 per cent of total return came from dividend income, the rest (£652) was capital growth, while *Lowland's* dividends accounted for 28 per cent of the total return, and capital growth accounted for 72 per cent. Interestingly *Lowland's* capital performance of £745 outdid that of *Greenfriar*.

FOLLOWING THE TREND

Burning the midnight oil poring over the performance tables is one thing, but what do they actually tell us?

The tables in Appendices 1 and 2 show the performance over one, three, five and ten years. At their crudest they allow you to pick out the trusts which have performed best over these different time scales.

It's unrealistic to expect investment trusts to always buck the market trend, but it's important to know which did better than average. There are several ways of doing this. The figures in this book give you a number of benchmarks against which you can compare investment trust performance. At the simplest you can see how well they did against the average of all investment trusts. You can then go on to see how well they did when compared to the market as a whole as measured by the various indices, such as the FT-Actuaries All Share Index, and the FT-Actuaries Investment Trust Index.

COMPARING LIKE WITH LIKE

Investment trusts don't all share the same investment objectives. Some are general trusts, others aim for capital growth, while others specialise in overseas markets, such as the United States or Japan, or market sectors such as technology or energy. Comparing a United States investment trust with one specialising in property shares is really a meaningless comparison.

This problem is solved by grouping investment trusts according to their investment objectives. Using this information, it's possible to see which sectors have done well, and which have lagged behind. You can compare United States and Japanese funds with their own stock market indices, and then within each category you can pick out those individual investment trusts which are doing well. The table opposite provides performance figures for a variety of standard indices.

The performance tables in the Appendices are ranged according to the 13 categories used by the AITC.

INDEX PERFORMANCE

At 31.12.87

	Price over:				Price total return over:			
Index	*1 year*	*3 years*	*5 years*	*10 years*	*1 year*	*3 years*	*5 years*	*10 years*
FTA INVESTMENT TRUST	89.4	136.2	217.1	374.3	91.1	145.3	245.0	512.4
UNIT HOLDER (UNIT TRUSTS)	NA	NA	NA	NA	94.3	137.8	202.9	344.8
FTA ALL SHARE	104.2	146.8	227.7	405.6	106.9	160.2	266.1	590.1
FT INDUSTRIAL ORDINARY	104.5	144.2	230.1	282.9	104.5	144.2	230.1	282.9
FTA BRITISH GOVT SECURITIES	104.4	106.5	106.4	111.1	111.8	132.1	154.5	244.0
STANDARD & POORS COMPOSITE	102.0	147.7	175.7	259.8	104.4	159.8	202.7	362.7
STANDARD & POORS COMPOSITE*	80.5	91.1	151.3	201.3	82.4	98.6	174.5	276.5
DOW JONES INDUSTRIAL	102.3	160.0	185.3	233.3	102.3	160.0	185.3	233.3
DOW JONES INDUSTRIAL*	80.7	98.7	159.5	180.7	80.7	98.7	159.5	180.7
TOKYO NEW STOCK EXCHANGE	110.9	188.9	290.7	474.0	111.4	192.1	300.4	517.3
TOKYO NEW STOCK EXCHANGE*	114.1	241.6	484.6	722.5	114.5	245.5	500.8	784.9
MS CAPITAL INT WORLD	114.3	217.9	262.9	376.0	116.3	231.9	296.6	508.6
MS CAPITAL INT WORLD*	90.2	134.4	226.4	291.3	91.8	143.1	255.3	388.1

* Adjusted for changes in exchange rates

Source: Nat West Wood Mackenzie

13 HOW TO CHOOSE AN INVESTMENT TRUST

Choosing an investment trust doesn't present the same kind of difficulties as choosing a unit trust. For a start, there are fewer of them. Investment trusts number around 200, of which only 150 or so merit serious attention, compared with over 1,000 unit trusts. In addition, the problem of selection isn't complicated by a proliferation of small specialist funds as is the case with unit trusts. Of course, there are specialist investment trusts, but by and large, investment trusts have stayed faithful to the idea that what investors want is professional investment management without the anxiety of having to decide for themselves which sector has the greatest potential.

This is not to say that choosing an investment trust presents no challenge. It does, but on the whole it's an enjoyable one, and really none too daunting.

METHODS OF INVESTMENT ANALYSIS

There are almost as many ways of looking at investment trusts as there are investment trusts. The main methods are considered briefly below.

Backing management

One method is to examine the track record of the trust managers. Most investment trusts are managed alongside others by firms of investment managers. Is there any evidence that some investment managers do better than others, or are most investment managers good in some areas, and poor in others? A few investment trusts are independent, employing their own investment managers – does this approach bring better results? The cult of the individual fund manager hasn't yet hit the world of investment trusts. Nonetheless, talent spotting might lead you to the winning investment trusts.

Backing the winners – or backing the losers

Another method is to analyse the performance statistics. Is an investment trust with a good long-term record likely to be the best bet in the future? Or are you more likely to make money if you take the counter-cyclical view and put your money in one of last year's losers? Or is this a strategy which only works with specialist funds?

Small trusts versus large trusts

Investment trusts range in size from around £1 billion to just over £1 million. There is a view that large trusts can become unwieldy and bureaucratic – a large ship awkward to manoeuvre in stormy seas. In contrast, small trusts can move more quickly and less obtrusively. Are these just stereotypes, or is there really a tendency for small trusts to perform better than large ones?

Reading the charts

There is a school of investment analysis which uses charts as a guide to buying and selling shares. Charts can be applied to investment trusts, just like any other share. The chartist draws a graph showing how an investment trust's shares have moved over a number of years. Chartists believe that shares follow certain predictable patterns and that by 'reading' the chart you can get an idea if a share is likely to rise or fall. Some specialist analysts use only charts, others dismiss them as hocus pocus, while many take the middle ground, and use them as an investment tool along with other techniques.

Crunching the numbers

Investment analysis is becoming less and less of an art and more and more of a science. There is now a whole younger generation of investment analysts and backroom computer boffins who can't see a share price without wanting to turn it into a ratio. Investment trusts are particularly amenable to mathematical analysis. At its simplest, the aim of all this number crunching is to try to quantify risk. Do all these ratios just confuse the issue or are they giving us fresh insights into how investment trusts can be expected to perform in the future?

In the next few chapters we look at how the big City stockbrokers go about the job of analysing investment trusts, and how in most cases you can do it for yourself.

14 BACKING MANAGEMENT

Times have changed since investment trusts were independent companies each with its own separate management. Today, most investment trusts are run as part of a stable by large investment management groups. There are some 26 management groups with responsibility for more than one investment trust, and three of them, Robert Fleming, Ivory & Sime and Touche Remnant, each manage 10 or more investment trusts.

Is there anything to be gained by looking at how the individual management groups have performed? Do some have a better record than others? Are some groups good at achieving above average results across a broad range of different types of investment trust? Is it possible to identify groups which appear to have lost their way?

MEASURING MANAGEMENT SKILL

Investment managers can't be held responsible for the size of the discount on investment trust shares. But they can be judged by how well they manage the investments in their care. The best way of judging the skills of the investment manager is to look at the performance figures for net asset value and net asset value total return. Net asset value measures capital performance; net asset value total return measures capital performance plus after-tax dividend income.

The figures in Appendix 3 list investment trusts by investment management group. The figures show the performance of net asset value and net asset value total return over one year, three years and seven years to the end of December 1987. They give the average performance of the groups as a whole, as well as of the individual trusts.

What do these figures tell us? To start with they can't tell us everything, and they must be read in combination with some of the other things we know about the management groups.

Large group performance

If everything else were equal, the investment management groups with a large number of trusts under management would seem likely to produce a performance very similar to the average of all trusts. Looking at the big three, Robert Fleming, Ivory & Sime and Touche Remnant, this only seems to be true in the case of Robert Fleming.

Ivory & Sime and Touche Remnant have both performed worse than average, Ivory & Sime considerably so.

The conclusions to be drawn from these figures coincide with how the City rates these three big investment houses. Robert Fleming is generally seen as sound and competent. Touche Remnant is seen as under seige and vulnerable to predators, where top management changes at the end of 1983 still haven't made an impact on investment performance. Ivory & Sime, based in Edinburgh, and having played an important part in the early financing of North Sea oil, is now regarded as having lost its way. Ivory & Sime responded in January 1988 with some very complicated proposals for restructuring three of their investment trusts: *Atlantic Assets, Edinburgh American Assets* and *Japan Assets*. These didn't find favour with investors, and the schemes put forward for *Atlantic Assets* and *Japan Assets* got the thumbs-down.

Medium and small group performance

It is harder to draw firm conclusions from the performance of the medium and small investment groups. Many of them run one or more specialist investment trusts, and if these areas have performed badly it can have a disproportionate effect on the performance of the whole group.

Foreign & Colonial, who run five trusts including one of the largest of them all, have until recently consistently managed to achieve above-average results across the board. This is no mean achievement, given the size of Foreign & Colonial itself, whose assets stood at around £235 million at the end of 1987. The results over the last year or so have been slightly disappointing.

It is far too early to say that Foreign & Colonial has lost its touch. The poor recent performance of almost all European investment trusts, *F & C Eurotrust* included, coupled with the one investment trust which might have been expected to have done better, *F & C Pacific*, goes some way to explain this slight fall from grace. However Foreign & Colonial is not confined to investment in Europe and the Far East as the *Foreign & Colonial* trust is a general trust with a worldwide spread of investments.

Japanese and Far Eastern investment trusts have an outstanding record, so much so that the presence of one or two such funds in an investment manager's stable of investment trusts can sometimes disguise a poor performance elsewhere. Scottish fund managers Baillie Gifford, for example, have done well with their two Japanese investment trusts, but haven't found much recent form with most of their others, such as *Mid Wynd International, Monks* and *Scottish Mortgage* .

The reverse is the case at Edinburgh Fund Managers. Here a lacklustre performance from most of their investment trusts serves to disguise the achievement of its one outstanding fund, *Crescent Japan,* the second oldest specialist Japanese investment trust.

Crescent Japan's great rival, *GT Japan*, belongs to a group which can point to a much more consistent record across the board. GT's two international growth investment trusts are normally among the best performers in their sector. *Nordic*, which specialises in the Scandinavian stock markets, and *United States Debenture Corporation*, which in June 1987 contracted to around a quarter of its previous size when it partially unitised, are the only blemishes on GT's outstanding record.

Gartmore's policy of developing specialist trusts has not provided very promising overall results. In fact, Gartmore do much better with their more general funds, such as *London & Strathclyde* and *Meldrum*. However, having said that, Gartmore's Scottish subsidiary did well when they turned *Scottish National* into a split capital investment trust, defying the critics who said it wasn't possible to do it with a large investment trust.

Among the medium-sized investment management groups, two names predominate. Henderson Administration and MIM both achieve good results across the whole range of their investment trusts, even though they pursue different policies.

Henderson are one of the best general fund managers in the business. Shares in their two outstanding long-term performers, *Lowland* and *Greenfriar,* are very tightly held, and difficult for the big institutions to deal in. But this is no problem for the private shareholder who is only interested in buying, say, £1,000 worth. Henderson only seem to lose their grip when they step into unfamiliar specialist territory. *Strata,* an investment trust they launched in 1985 to specialise in smaller companies, has not done well in what has been an outstanding sector.

MIM have a very different approach. They are the specialists par excellence, and as luck or judgement would have it, MIM have specialised in three areas where investment trusts have achieved great success – Japan and the Far East, smaller companies, and split capital trusts. With *Consolidated Venture* they have even done well running an investment trust specialising in the high risk area of venture capital.

Don't overlook individual excellence

There are disadvantages to trying to assess the management group across the range of its activities. You might end up disregarding investment managers whose overall record is poor, but who run one or two really outstanding funds, as is the case with Edinburgh Fund Managers. There is also a tendency to overlook those managers who look after just one investment trust, or where the trust does its own management independently.

On this basis it would be easy to miss the likes of *Temple Bar,* a medium-sized mainly UK investment trust managed by Guinness Mahon. And there is *Globe,* the largest trust of all with net assets of £862 million at the end of 1987, which still manages an above-average performance. In among Kleinwort Grieveson's stable of investment trusts there is *Kleinwort Smaller Companies,* a gem which has done well in a top performing sector, while the performance of the Throgmorton group including the top trusts *Throgmorton USM* and the longer-standing *Throgmorton Trust* is dragged down by the unfortunate *Alva,* which Throgmorton only started managing in 1986. And among the independents you might fail to spot *Moorgate* .

Having said that, there is no doubt that looking at the overall performance of management does have its uses. After all it is no bad thing if it leads the investment trust novice to the likes of Foreign & Colonial, Henderson Administration, and Throgmorton. They could be in far worse hands.

FOLLOWING THE INDIVIDUAL MANAGER

The cult of the individual fund manager has not yet hit the world of investment trusts, and there are probably good reasons why it never will. This is very different from unit trusts, where managers do move around and their reputations and investors go with them.

In the year or so before Big Bang, whole teams of investment analysts were bought and sold and 'golden handcuffed' to their desks in an amazing game of musical chairs. But although stockbrokers' analysts use the same skills, the world of investment trusts remained relatively untouched by that period of madness.

Following the fortunes of an individual investment trust manager through various job changes is almost unknown. The explanation is not hard to find. Unlike unit trusts, investment trusts are quoted companies. This imposes rather more responsibilities on their managers and directors than is generally required of unit trusts.

The average investment trust is larger than the average unit trust, and investment trust managers are likely to be in a much more senior position within their firm than most unit trust managers. By the time someone is given their own investment trust to run, they have probably reached a level at which they have made a lifetime commitment to a particular investment trust or firm of investment managers.

This is not to say that the work of individual investment managers goes unnoticed in the City. It's just that the public is largely unaware of the reputations of the people responsible for running investment trusts.

But whenever individual investment trust managers are mentioned certain names keep recurring. People like Grant Cochrane, of Dunedin, Max Ward at Baillie Gifford, John Walton at British Empire, Michael Hart at Foreign & Colonial, Colin Black and Jimmy West at Globe, Hugh Priestley and Richard Smith at Henderson, Peter Knapton at Temple Bar, Bob Seabrook at Throgmorton, Peter Rintoul at Grahams Rintoul, Philip Henderson at Ensign and Matthew Oakeshott at Value & Income all emerge as names to watch.

THE FLAGSHIP FUND

There is another school of thought which believes that if you look for the flagship fund within any particular fund management group, you will probably find it is being run by the group's best investment manager. There is something to be said for the theory. It may not lead you to the most exciting investment trusts, but it is certainly true there are few real duds among the flagship funds.

Flagship funds which have done well are *Foreign & Colonial*, Henderson's *Witan*, Ivory & Sime's *British Assets*, Kleinwort's *Charter*, Martin Currie's *Securities Trust of Scotland*, and *Throgmorton*, while Baillie Gifford's *Scottish Mortgage*, Fleming *Mercantile*, Gartmore's *English & Scottish*, and Martin Currie's other flagship, *Scottish Eastern, Murray International* and Dunedin's *Edinburgh Investment* have all turned in respectable performances.

But, like all good theories, there are the exceptions. Kleinwort's other big investment trust, *Overseas, Govett Strategic* and *TR Industrial & General* all have performance records well below the average.

15 BACKING INDIVIDUAL TRUSTS

There is a theory of investment management which says that instead of wasting your time analysing shares, you are likely to do equally well choosing them with a pin. And instead of actively managing them, you are likely to do just as well if you forget all about them.

Certainly, anyone who has acquired a portfolio of shares knows how difficult it is to have them all performing well. There are always those dead certs which turn out to be real duds. And the high dealing costs associated with actively managing a portfolio can eat into profits.

A policy of random selection and laissez-faire may have much to recommend it once you have built up a portfolio of shares – it is, after all, just another way of spreading risk. However, anyone just starting out as a stock market investor can't afford to put all their eggs in just one or two baskets – the risk of them all turning bad is just too great.

Investment trusts save you the chore of researching individual shares. But you then have the problem of choosing an investment trust which has a better than average chance of doing well. Looking at how the management groups perform is one pointer. The next step is to look at the individual trusts. You need to know:

a) how well the investment trust has performed; and

b) the size of the discount.

Studying the performance tables gives you the benefit of hindsight, but they cannot foretell the future. Having said that, the performance tables are the stock-in-trade of the investment trust analyst, so don't disdain them, because they can yield a lot of useful information. There is a very wide difference in performance between the very best trusts and the worst. For example over the ten years to the end of December 1987, £1,000 invested in *Lowland,* the top performing investment trust covered by the NatWest Wood Mackenzie figures, produced a total return (share price rise plus dividend income) of £15,354, whereas the worst, *Viking Resources,* produced just £1,868. The average was £5,381. Ten years is, of course, a long time, but even a year can throw up wide differences in performance. For example in 1987, £1,000 invested in the best trust, *Welsh Industrial,* produced a total return of £2,045, while the worst, *F & C Eurotrust,* fell to just £479. The average was £901.

The returns produced by the best investment trusts look tempting. But in reality, however much time you spend researching the performance tables, your chances of choosing one of the top performing trusts are probably not great. What you can hope to do is choose a trust which does better than average. And if you do you should be well satisfied.

IS PERFORMANCE A GOOD GUIDE?

Is there any point in choosing an investment trust on the basis of its past performance? The answer appears to be a guarded yes, and backing past winners is probably as good a way as any other of increasing your chances of doing well.

Stockbrokers Warburg Securities have come to this conclusion after looking at the subsequent behaviour of top performing investment trusts. They took the best investment trusts over the three-year period to June 1986, and measured their performance over the following year. The top 50 went up by an average of 72 per cent, compared with 50 per cent for the rest. The top 20 increased by 78 per cent, while the rest went up by 54 per cent. The top ten produced an increase of 82 per cent, compared with 51 per cent for the rest.

The stockbrokers then looked at the best performing investment trusts in the year to June 1986, to see if one-year performance was any guide to likely future performance. On this basis the evidence is less conclusive, although the top trusts did still go on to produce a superior performance, even though the differences were less remarkable.

The discount

Most investment trusts stand at a discount to their net asset value. And in theory at least, the bigger the discount, the cheaper the shares. Looking at the discount, and trying to discover which trusts look cheap for no good reason, is a time-honoured method of choosing an investment trust. But is there any evidence that it works? The existence of a big discount doesn't necessarily mean that a trust is undervalued. It may be standing on a big discount because the managers aren't doing a very good job, or it might be in an out-of-fashion sector with few immediate prospects.

Even if you do manage to find a genuinely undervalued investment trust, the narrowing of the discount from, say, 25 per cent to 10 per cent is likely over a ten-year period to account for only a small part of your total return, and in the meantime you may have missed out on better investment opportunities because you focused on the discount.

Active investment trust investors may be able to make money playing the discounts, i.e. buying a share when the discount is high, in the hope that it will narrow quickly and they can make a quick turn. And according to Warburg Securities, there is evidence that investment trusts with big discounts can expect those discounts to narrow by a greater percentage than those standing on average or below average discounts.

Nonetheless, the discount game is probably best left to the professional investor who doesn't mind occasionally taking a short-term view. But for the private investor the movement in the discount is generally not large enough to justify the dealing cost. This is not to say that you should ignore the discount altogether. By all means take it into consideration, but don't let it be the only determining factor in your choice.

IS SIZE IMPORTANT?

The world of investment is full of theories, many of which are almost impossible to prove conclusively one way or the other. Many people expect small investment trusts to do better than large ones. If this is the case, you would stand a better chance of choosing a top performer if you plumped for a small investment trust.

The argument is persuasive. Large trusts are seen as lumbering giants, difficult to manoeuvre in fast changing markets. For example, if a large trust wants to bump up its liquidity, it usually has to sell stock to do it. And the slightest hint that one of the big investment trusts is changing tack can move the market against it.

By contrast, the theory is that small investment trusts can be swifter on their feet and less conspicuous: but is there any truth in it?

The answer is not much, and in fact, many large trusts can point to very good long-term performance figures. Looking at the 25 largest investment trusts in the AITC at the end of 1986, eight were among the top quarter of all investment trusts in the previous one and three years. But when you look at the smallest 25, only six did as well over the same periods.

There are several reasons which go some way to explaining why large trusts on balance do better than small ones. Firstly, the management charges on large trusts are likely to absorb a smaller percentage of the revenue. Management charges vary from as little as 0.2 per cent of assets to over 5 per cent. Over the long term, the size of the management charge can have a significant effect on performance.

Then there is the flagship theory. As explained in the last chapter, investment managers running a whole stable of investment trusts may put more effort into managing their biggest investment trust. This is often seen as the flagship, the one against which the whole group is judged.

LAST YEAR'S DUDS, THIS YEAR'S STARS

Many investors are convinced that you can do well by taking the counter-cyclical view and putting money in last year's poor performers in the hope that they will miraculously emerge as tomorrow's winners. Some people claim this is the only way of making money out of unit trusts. On the stock market, gambling on penny shares is a variation on the same theme. But does it work for investment trusts? Do you have a good chance of doing well if you put your money in one of the worst performing investment trusts? In this case the answer is a fairly firm no, and the reason is not hard to find. It's a theory which may work, at least to a limited extent, where there are a large number of specialist funds, as is the case with unit trusts. The performance of specialist funds is often a feast to famine business – one year a particular speciality or market does well, only to then fall from grace.

In spite of the increasing number of specialist investment trusts, the proportion is still small, and investors can't expect an above average performance if they choose one of the worst performers. The notable exception is some of the Japanese funds. Anyone who put their money into Japanese investment trusts at the end of 1985, when the Japanese funds were among the year's worst performers, would have gone on to do exceptionally well.

COMPARING SECTOR PERFORMANCE

The AITC places their members into categories according to their investment policy (see Chapter 7). This gives you one further way of looking at investment trust performance and is a useful way of narrowing down your choice.

The breakdown illustrates which sectors have shown the others a clean pair of heels and which are bringing up the rear, and within each sector you can see which individual trusts have done best.

Most of the sectors have a performance which hovers around the average. Nonetheless, the categories are still useful. For example you might be looking for an investment trust with a low yield, so you could restrict your search to investment trusts in one of the sectors offering capital growth. On the other hand, you may be looking for a high income, in which case you will probably find what you want among the income funds. Appendix 1 gives details of most investment trusts with their AITC sector.

There are, however, several sectors which have done particularly well, and others which have done notably worse than average. The North American and the commodity and energy funds are the worst laggards. For example, £1,000 invested at the end of December 1977 in the average North American investment trust produced a total return (share price plus net dividend reinvested) of £3,206, compared with £5,381 for the average of all investment trusts. The commodity and energy investment trusts did even worse. Here £1,000 invested in December 1977 had grown to only £2,671 ten years later.

As already mentioned, the outstanding performers are the Japanese, the capital shares of split capital trusts and, to a lesser extent, those invested in the smaller companies. Again, looking at the same ten-year period, £1,000 invested in the average Japanese investment trust produced £8,200; in the average capital share £7,518 and in the average smaller companies trust £6,411.

16 READING THE CHARTS AND RATIOS

There are a lot of performance figures for investment trusts – figures for net assets, figures for share performance, figures for dividend growth. With so much raw material to work on, it's perhaps surprising that it has taken the big City stockbrokers so long to harness the science of the statistician and the computer boffin. But in the post-Big Bang City, the climate is now changing. Technical and mathematical analysis is being taken a lot more seriously, and investment trusts are getting the treatment.

CHARTS

Charts are the one area of technical analysis which has been around for a long time. The chartist plots the performance of a particular share and that of a comparable index on a chart; he or she believes that the share price incorporates everything that everyone knows about a certain share at any point in time, and that investor sentiment often follows a predictable course.

The chartist uses these share price patterns to try to predict the future course of the share price, looking for certain set patterns which can often be an indication that a share price may be on the threshold of moving up or down.

But charts can also be used in much simpler ways. A chart can show you how well a share has performed relative to an index. If, for example, it has consistently underperformed the market, the share analyst must justify any decision to invest in that company. There is a lot of mumbo-jumbo surrounding chart analysis, and many exaggerated claims have been made for it in the past. Nowadays, few people subscribe to the theory that all you need to do is look at the charts and you will end up making a killing on the stock market. This is not to say that no one consults them any more. Many stockbrokers use charts, but they do so in conjunction with other methods.

There are two firms which specialise in producing charts: Chart Analysis and Investment Research of Cambridge. Neither produce many charts for investment trusts because they say that, until recently, their clients, mainly City institutions and firms of stockbrokers, have not asked for them.

Chart Analysis produces charts on *Atlantic Assets, Anglo & Overseas, Alliance, Electra, Foreign & Colonial, Fleming Mercantile, British Assets, British Investment Trust, Edinburgh Investment Trust,*

TR Technology, TR Industrial, Securities Trust of Scotland, Globe, Scottish Mortgage, and *Scottish American.* Investment Reseach of Cambridge only do charts on *Edinburgh Investment Trust* and *Atlantic Assets.*

Chart Analysis produces a book of 700 charts. To subscribe to the service even only once a month costs £380 a year. Not many private investors could justify the expense, so if you are interested in charts and you have a friendly stockbroker, ask them if they produce charts on the investment trust or trusts you are considering investing in. If you want to get in touch with Chart Analysis, their address is 7 Swallow Street, London W1R 7HD; tel: 01-439 4961. And if you want to learn more, they recommend a book: 'Technical Analysis Explained', by Martin Pring, published by McGraw-Hill, price £49.95.

USING RATIOS

Performance figures can tell you a lot. They show you how a particular investment trust has done over the period you have chosen to measure it. If you think of an investment trust taking a journey from point A to point B, performance figures show you the result of that journey. What they don't show is the route it took to arrive at point B.

Two investment trusts can take entirely different routes, but both end up at the same point B. One investment trust may have shown a steady pattern closely mirroring the market as a whole, the other may have jumped around, following a much more volatile course. But if both these trusts start and finish their journey at the same place, does it matter what happens in between? This depends on your temperament as an investor. If it will give you endless sleepless nights to see your investment trust rise and fall sharply at the slightest provocation, you would obviously be happier in one which shows a steadier pattern.

On the other hand, if you like the idea of a stormy ride, or are thinking of taking out a regular savings scheme (see the theory of pound-cost averaging in Chapter 20) you might be better off with a more volatile trust.

BETA FACTORS

Beta factors are the best-known method of measuring volatility. On the face of it, betas look complicated. However, you don't need to know how to work them out for yourself – all you need to know is what they measure and what they mean. Betas measure how a share performed compared to a relevant market index. A share whose performance exactly matched the index has a beta of 1.0. A beta above 1.0 indicates that the share is more volatile than the market: one below 1.0 that it is less volatile. This is how it works, and the formula can be applied to investment trust asset values just as easily as share prices. If the index moves up from 100 to 110 in a month, that's a rise of 10 per cent. If the share you are following goes up from 100p to 115p, that's a rise of 15 per cent – 50 per cent better than the index. And if during the following month the index drops by 10 per cent, and your share falls by 15 per cent, it has fallen 50 per cent further than the index. This gives a beta of 1.5 which is an indication that the share is more volatile than the comparable index. Compare this with another share which only goes up to 107.5p when the index rises from 100 to 110, underperforming the market by a quarter. If it showed a similar pattern when the market went down, and failed to fall as far as the index, it would have a beta of 0.75.

Stockbrokers Warburg Securities calculate betas based on investment trust asset performance. Listed below are the investment trusts with the lowest betas – the least risky, and the highest betas – the most risky. The figures are as at the end of October 1987. The index used for comparison is the Morgan Stanley Capital International World Index.

Betas tell you what is likely to happen to investment trust asset values during the journey over time from A to B. What they don't tell you is what those asset values will be worth at point B. The three year rankings by asset performance given alongside the betas seem to indicate that you stand a better chance of doing well with an investment trust with a low risk beta than one showing a higher risk.

Trusts with the lowest betas

At 31.10.87

Investment trust	*Beta*	*Ranking**
Save and Prosper Linked	0.31	NA
Dundee & London	0.35	NA
Save & Prosper Return of Assets	0.44	NA
Northern Securities	0.48	26
Shires	0.50	83
Fulcrum	0.53	NA
Japan Assets	0.53	100
North British Canadian	0.56	6
New Tokyo	0.57	89
Moorgate	0.59	4
Murray Ventures	0.59	18
Kleinwort Smaller Companies	0.63	3
Fleming Mercantile	0.64	49
First Charlotte	0.66	81
Temple Bar	0.67	8
Baillie Gifford Japan	0.68	6
Baillie Gifford Technology	0.68	111
Ambrose	0.70	27
Berry	0.70	60
Drayton Consolidated	0.70	57
Personal Assets	0.70	NA

Guide to investment trusts

Investment trust	Beta	Ranking*
Throgmorton	0.70	7
City of Oxford	0.71	18
Drayton Far Eastern	0.71	18
London Atlantic	0.71	15
TR Property	0.71	25

* by three-year asset performance

Trusts with the highest betas

At 31.10.87

Investment trust	Beta	Ranking*
Marine Adventure Sailing	1.40	97
Child Health Research	1.35	96
Govett Oriental	1.27	37
TR Australia	1.23	113
Fleming American	1.19	109
Gartmore American	1.17	101
Govett Strategic	1.16	43
GT Japan	1.09	35
Jove	1.08	NA
TR Pacific Basin	1.08	76
Murray Smaller Markets	1.07	29
TR Natural Resources	1.07	112
Fleming Far Eastern	1.06	33
Fleming Universal	1.05	80
Precious Metals	1.05	57
North Atlantic Securities	1.05	98
Govett Atlantic	1.04	103
Greenfriar	1.04	30
American	1.03	104
Fleming Overseas	1.03	91
Independent	1.03	115
Romney	1.03	95
Electric & General	1.02	47
Witan	1.01	38
Edinburgh American	1.00	107
TR North American	1.00	107
Fleming Technology	1.00	105

* by three year asset performance

Sharpe ratios

There is now a ratio which attempts to combine risk and return. The Sharpe Ratio, named after Professor William Sharpe, can be used to show which investment trusts have earned the highest return while taking the least risk.

The investment trusts listed are those with the highest Sharpe ratios at the end of October 1987. These figures are based on 36 month performance figures and they show the investment trusts which have shown the highest return for the least possible risk over that period.

The list is as interesting for those that it leaves out as for those which are included. In spite of their good performance, Japanese investment trusts don't feature in the list, as their high volatility excludes them, while on this basis many of the capital shares of split capital trusts – traditionally thought of as a high-risk investment – can justify the risk by pointing to their high returns.

There are even a couple of investment trusts whose merits as measured by their Sharpe ratios seem to be totally ignored by the market. *Tor* and *Jove* were both standing at discounts well above average.

Warburg Securities are the only stockbrokers currently making available Sharpe ratios for investment trusts.These are worked out for them by US investment consultants, Newgate Management Associstes.To prove their usefulness, they looked at the investment trusts with the highest Sharpe ratios in June 1986. A year later, the 50 investment trusts with the highest Sharpe ratios had increased by 52 per cent compared with 53 per cent for the market as a whole – hardly convincing statistics, until you look at what happened to the top 20 and 10 investment trusts. The top 20 increased by 79 per cent. The top ten did even better, increasing by an average of 103 per cent.

Investment trusts with the highest Sharpe ratios

At 31.10.87 *Investment trust*	*Sharpe ratio*	*Discount to net assets*
Updown	0.48	NA
Fashion & General	0.38	NA
Archimedes	0.34	NA
Capital Gearing	0.34	NA
English National Deferred	0.34	+7.8
Kleinwort Smaller Companies	0.32	4.8
London Atlantic	0.32	8.3
Lowland	0.30	+15.4
North British Canadian	0.30	11.9

Investment trust	Sharpe ratio	Discount to net assets
M & G Dual	0.29	NA
Save & Prosper Linked	0.29	NA
Albany	0.27	NA
M & G Second Dual	0.27	NA
Murray Ventures	0.27	17.0
Scottish Cities	0.27	NA
Child Health Research	0.25	+44.0
City & Commercial	0.25	10.0
New Throgmorton (1983)	0.25	59.7
Greenfriar	0.24	+5.9
Jos Holdings	0.24	9.2
Tor	0.24	25.4
Trust of Property Shares	0.23	NA
Equity Consort Deferred	0.22	12.5
Gresham House	0.22	NA
Jove	0.22	31.6
Rights & Issues	0.22	NA
Dundee & London	0.21	NA
Fleming Fledgeling	0.21	7.6

Source: Warburg Securities

17 HOW TO READ THE REPORT AND ACCOUNTS

Investment trust reports and accounts are now much more informative than they used to be. There was a time when management companies took the view that the less shareholders knew the better.

The directors of public companies are legally required to send shareholders an annual report of their activities plus the accounts. Investment trusts are no exception, and nowadays the report and accounts is one of the best sources of information on individual investment trusts.

If you are a shareholder, you will get the annual report and accounts automatically, plus an interim statement halfway through the financial year. If you are not yet a shareholder, but would like to know more about a particular investment trust, most management companies are only too happy to send prospective investors a copy of the last annual report and accounts.

The format of annual reports varies from management company to management company. Some items are obligatory, others are at the discretion of the management. A good set of report and accounts should give you the following information:

- the Chairman's statement;

- the directors' annual review;

- an investment review;

- a list of investments and their value;

- the ten-year investment record along with some comparative data;

- a revenue statement;

- the balance sheet;

- a statement of the source and application of funds;

- the auditor's report.

EXAMINING A REPORT IN DETAIL

The Scottish Mortgage and Trust is one of the largest investment trusts. It is managed by Baillie Gifford, who put a lot of effort into their report and accounts, and it is a good example of what you can expect to find.

Scottish Mortgage ends its financial year on 31 March. The report and accounts for the year to the end of March 1987 begin with some information about the trust itself. This includes a statement of the investment aims, which are stated as follows: 'Its purpose is to achieve maximum growth in both capital values and dividends. It invests internationally, mainly in quoted securities. Its portfolio is concentrated in a relatively small number of holdings. These are mainly in strong businesses with good prospects of growth. Its managers are constantly alert for opportunities for major strategic moves'.

Then follows a table which compares *Scottish Mortgage*'s five year net asset and dividend growth with those investment trusts which fall into the same investment category as defined by the AITC.

CHAIRMAN'S STATEMENT

Scottish Mortgage's chairman, Sir Michael Herries, is a busy man. He is also chairman of The Royal Bank of Scotland, a director of Scottish Widows', the big Scottish life insurance company, and the overseas trader Jardine Matheson among others. He begins his Chairman's statement with a few financial highlights with comparative figures from the year before.

Highlights of Chairman's statement

Total assets	£638.0m	£491.6m
Debentures	£70.7m	£20.7m
Total net assets	£567.3m	£470.9m
Asset value per ordinary share*	783.8p	650.2p
Revenue before taxation	£10.65m	£10.02m
Earnings per oridinary share	10.26p	9.27p
Dividends per ordinary share	10.00p	8.50p

*after deducting prior changes at par

This gives the bare bones of the year's achievements. The value of *Scottish Mortgage*'s investments – this is the figure shown under the heading 'total assets' – rose by 30 per cent to £638 million. But from the shareholder's point of view, the most important figure is the net asset value. This is the amount which effectively belongs to the shareholders. It is worked out by deducting any borrowings from total assets. In the case of *Scottish Mortgage*, net assets rose by 20 per cent to £567.3 million, rather less than the rise in total assets. This occurred because *Scottish Mortgage* increased its borrowings from £20.7 million to £70.7 million with an issue of £50 million of 6-12 per cent Stepped Interest Debenture Stock.

The asset value per ordinary share is the net asset value which can be attributed to each ordinary share. It is arrived at by dividing the net asset value by the number of shares in issue. As no new shares were issued during the year, the increase in assets per share – from 650.2p to 783.8p – is 20 per cent, matching the increase in net assets. The difference between an investment trust's net asset value per share and its share price is the discount or premium.

Revenue before taxation is the income *Scottish Mortgage* received in dividends and interest during the year. Earnings per ordinary share shows the amount of revenue attributable to each ordinary share. The amount rose by 10.7 per cent to 10.26p per share, of which 10p was paid to *Scottish Mortgage* shareholders as dividends.

Sir Michael Herries continues his report with an outline of the year's investment strategy. The proceeds of the issue of debenture stock were invested mainly in UK quoted convertible stocks, and this produced more than enough income to cover the interest payments on the debentures.

Baillie Gifford's investment trust savings and dividend reinvestment schemes are also detailed.

WHERE THE MONEY IS INVESTED

Baillie Gifford list *Scottish Mortgage*'s individual investments in a separate list tucked into a flap at the end of the report and accounts. The report itself includes a couple of segment charts. The first shows where the money is invested geographically with a figure in brackets for the previous year, the other, where the money is invested by broad market sectors such as consumer goods, capital goods and financial services, again with the figures for previous years shown in brackets.

From these, investors can see there was a slight switch in emphasis out of Japan and the United States and into the UK and Europe.

There is also a more detailed breakdown of the trust's investments by market sector, with consumer goods, for example, split into nine separate categories, from light electrical to food to healthcare.

The investment managers also account for themselves. 'A year ago we were unenthusiastic about prospects for investment in the United States. In the event this has turned out to be correct.' This is how Baillie Gifford began their review of the United States market. Each geographical area gets its own write-up, where the managers explain their investment philosophy, and in some cases even their reasons for holding individual shares.

STATISTICS

The annual report and accounts is always a good place to find facts and figures about your investment trust. *Scottish Mortgage* include a ten-year record of the trust's income and capital performance. From this you can see that the dividends per share rose from 3p in 1977 to 10p in 1987, and that asset value per share rose from 139.2p to 783.8p.

THE DIRECTORS' REPORT

All company reports and accounts must include a directors' report. It is here that certain official business is conducted, and they usually make for dreary reading. But don't ignore them. Important details are often hidden away in the directors' report and it can be important not to miss them. Here you will find how many shares the directors own; whether there are any substantial outside shareholders who own more than five per cent of the shares; and any proposed changes in the company's capital structure.

The directors' report is often the source of questions at a company's annual meeting. After all, if the directors have been selling their shares you might want to know why. Likewise, if someone has been building up a big share stake, you might want to know if the management knows of their intentions towards your company.

THE ACCOUNTS

There are three elements to the accounts of an investment trust:

a) the revenue account;

b) the balance sheet; and

c) the source and application of funds.

It is important to read all three in conjunction with the notes to the accounts which help explain the figures. For *Scottish Mortgage*, these three parts of the accounts are shown at the end of this chapter.

Many people panic when they first look at a set of accounts. That initial fear never leaves some people, which is a pity, because investment trust accounts are much easier to read than most company accounts, and they are full of interesting information.

The revenue account

The revenue account shows you how much income the investment trust earned during the financial year in question and how it went about spending it. The figures for the previous year are shown for comparison.

The revenue account for *Scottish Mortgage* shows that income increased by more than £3 million to £16.8 million in the year to the end of March 1987. During the year *Scottish Mortgage* raised £50 million with an issue of debentures. This money had been invested and was already producing a stream of dividend income – hence the big leap in investment income.

But by the same token, the amount of interest *Scottish Mortgage* had to pay out had also shot up. In fact, it nearly doubled from £2.6 million to £5.1 million. However, the impact of the new issue of debentures on the revenue account was still favourable, with net revenue after tax and preference share dividends up from £6.7 million to £7.4 million.

The surplus after paying ordinary shareholders their dividends is then added to the accumulated revenue reserve and carried over into the balance sheet.

The notes to the revenue account reveal a few interesting details. For example, in a busy year for corporate activity, underwriting income rose from £307,000 to £583,000. Underwriting is the practice whereby the big city institutions guarantee to buy a new issue of company shares at a certain price for a fixed fee.

Another note gave the chairman's fee as £5,000 with the directors each receiving £4,000.

The balance sheet

The balance sheet is a snapshot in time. Taken once a year – on the last day of the financial year – the balance sheet tells you how much a company is worth. For an investment trust, the balance sheet is the single most important financial document, the one you need to study to understand how the net asset value is arrived at.

The net asset value of an investment trust is the market value of all its investments plus any bank deposits, after deducting all borrowings, be they short-term bank borrowings, or long-term debt such as debentures and loan stocks.

Taking the example of *Scottish Mortgage*, the balance sheet starts with the value of the underlying investments. These stood at £639 million on 31 March 1987, up from £481 million a year earlier. So even allowing for the extra influx of funds from the £50 million issue of debenture stock, the value of the underlying investments showed a healthy increase.

The assets are now adjusted by what are known as 'net current assets' or, in this case, liabilities. Current assets are amounts which are owed to the company at some stage within the next year. Short-term bank deposits are included here.

Current liabilities are the opposite. They are amounts the company must pay out within the next year, and this is where you find any bank overdrafts.

With many companies, these figures can be a very important pointer to how well the company is controlling its cash flow. For investment trusts they don't have the same significance. Read them with the accompanying notes just in case they throw up anything interesting. The *Scottish Mortgage* balance sheet shows net current liabilities of just over £1 million, which is deducted from fixed assets, to give a figure of £638 million for total assets.

The figures appear to have little in common with those for the previous year, but then there is no particular reason why they should have. For example, one of the biggest elements in the figure for debtors is the amount of money caught up in the settlement pipeline. On the 1987 balance sheet date, £2.5 million of shares had been sold, but the money had not yet been received. A year earlier the figure was much higher at £10 million.

Having arrived at a figure for total assets you are normally but one short step away from arriving at net asset value – this magical figure which actually tells you how much your investment is in fact worth. For some investment trusts, the figure for total assets and net assets are one and the same thing. But many investment trusts have some long-term borrowings, in which case these must be deducted from total assets to get a figure for net assets.

Scottish Mortgage's balance sheet shows creditors of £70.7 million. This is where you find the long-term borrowings. The notes list £20 million of 8.14 per cent stepped interest debenture stock 2020, £50 million of 6.12 per cent stepped interest debenture stock 2026 and £675,000 of 4.5 per cent irredeemable debenture stock.

As we have already seen in the part of the report showing the year's highlights, *Scottish Mortgage*'s long-term debt rose by £50 million during the year to the end of March 1987, as a result of that new issue of debentures. But even allowing for this, net assets rose from £471 million to £567 million. Capital and reserves show how those net assets were financed. The total figure is the same as for net assets. The two must balance – hence the name balance sheet. In the case of investment trusts, net assets are financed by the ordinary and preference shares. To this is added all the accumulated net gains (gains less losses) made on the sale of investments, plus any net gains on investments still held in the portfolio, and then finally there is the addition of the revenue reserve transferred from the revenue account.

The source and application of funds

The source and application of funds combines information from the revenue account and the balance sheet. It is the company's cash flow statement and, as its name implies, it tells you where the company got its money during the year and how it spent it. With most companies, the source and application of funds is the quickest and easiest way of gauging the health of a company.

It doesn't assume quite the same importance for investment trusts. However, it does provide one very useful piece of information. It tells you how actively the investment trust's funds have been managed. This is often called 'churning', i.e. how often the investments are turned over or churned. It is often argued that investment managers should be obliged to measure their performance each year against the performance they would have achieved if they had actually done nothing and just sat on their hands all year.

Taking the case of *Scottish Mortgage* the source and application of funds statement shows the investments were actively managed during the year. Nearly £303 million of investments were sold and another £359 million were bought, compared with total investments of £639 million. This is higher than many other trusts. For example, *TR City of London*, with total investments of £198 million at the end of June 1987, sold investments worth £48.6 million and bought others for £47.6 million during the previous year – a much lower level of turnover.

Revenue account for the year to 31 March 1987

	1987 £,000	1986 £,000
INCOME		
Income from investments	15,512	11,682
Interest receivable and other income	1,305	1,847
Gross income	16,817	13,529
EXPENSES		
Interest payable	(5,088)	(2,600)
	11,729	10,929
Administrative expenses	(1,081)	(904)
REVENUE		
from ordinary activities before taxation	10,648	10,025
Tax on revenue from ordinary activities	(3,182)	(3,273)
REVENUE		
from ordinary activities after taxation	7,466	6,752
DIVIDENDS		
Preference paid	(67)	(67)
	7,399	6,685
Ordinary paid and proposed	(7,214)	(6,133)
ACCUMULATED REVENUE		
Net revenue for the financial year	185	552
Brought forward	6,958	6,406
Carried forward	7,143	6,958
EARNINGS		
per ordinary share	10.26p	9.27p

Balance sheet at 31 March 1987

	1987 £,000	£,000	1986 £,000	£,000
FIXED ASSETS				
Investments		639,085		480,931
CURRENT ASSETS				
Debtors	4,387		10,715	
Investments	8,550		18,578	
Cash at bank and in hand	2,441		4,781	
	15,378		34,074	
CREDITORS				
Amounts falling due				
within one year	(16,463)		(23,386)	
NET CURRENT				
(LIABILITIES)/ASSETS		(1,085)		10,688
TOTAL ASSETS				
less current liabilities		638,000		491,619
CREDITORS				
Amounts falling due after				
more than one year		(70,675)		(20,675)
PROVISIONS FOR LIABILITIES				
AND CHARGES				
Deferred taxation		–		(14)
		567,325		470,930
CAPITAL AND RESERVES				
Called up share capital		19,911		19,911
Capital reserve		394,721		264,803
Unrealised appreciation		145,550		179,258
Accumulated revenue		7,143		6,958
		567,325		470,930

Source and application of funds for the year to 31 March 1987

	1987 £,000	£,000	1986 £,000	£,000
REVENUE				
Source of funds –				
Revenue from ordinary activities				
before taxation		10,648		10,025
Application of funds –				
Taxation paid and suffered on income	3,571		2,559	
Dividends paid	6,416		5,478	
		9,987		8,037
Increase in revenue funds		661		1,988
CAPITAL				
Source of funds –				
Sales of short-dated government				
securities	–		16,421	
Sales of bonds	–		4,898	
Sales of currency options	–		4,345	
Sales of other securities:				
United Kingdom	132,153		74,849	
United States	49,400		58,542	
Europe	15,303		7,528	
Japan	102,316		20,869	
Other countries	3,809		3,954	
New debenture stock	50,000		–	
Profit on forward exchange contract	–		–	
		352,981		202,588
Application of funds –				
Purchase of currency options		–		1,088
Purchases of other securities :				
United Kingdom	189,360		47,637	
United States	69,582		72,902	
Europe	48,411		43,406	
Japan	40,261		26,704	
Other countries	11,521		150	
Repayment of bank loans	–		10,761	
Repayment of debentures	–		551	
Realised currency loss	866		(815)	
Items not involving movement				
of funds	4,655		400	
Previous year tax adjustment	105		–	
		364,761		202,784

Contd

	1987 £,000	£,000	1986 £,000	£,000
Decrease in capital funds		(11,780)		(196)
Total increase (decrease) in working capital		(11,119)		1,792
Represented by :				
Increase (decrease) in debtors	(6,400)		(6,498)	
Decrease (increase) in creditors	11,976		(13,045)	
Increase (decrease) in cash	(6,667)		4,220	
Increase (decrease) in short-term deposits	(10,028)		4,119	
		(11,119)		1,792

18 WHERE TO GO FOR INFORMATION

Investment trusts are always hitting the headlines. Hardly a week passes without news of a takeover bid, a reorganisation, or the emergence of a big share stake. Anyone wanting to keep track of all these developments has their work cut out.

There is no shortage of information on investment trusts, but even if you are a regular reader of the financial pages in the newspapers you need to know where to start.

THE AITC FIGURES

News of wheeling and dealing, or even reports of annual results, are all very well. What they don't tell you is how to locate the investment trusts with the best investment record. Seasoned investment trust investors have the second Saturday in the month noted for months ahead in their diaries. This is the day the AITC publishes performance figures for most of their member companies in the *Daily Telegraph*. The figures show how some 140 investment trusts performed over one, three and five years. To make the figures comparable with those produced for unit trusts, the AITC figures show share price performance with an amount reinvested for after tax dividends. There is also a figure for yield.

Unfortunately, the figures aren't comprehensive. Not all AITC members subscribe to the service, and non-members wouldn't be included anyway. It means that investment trusts such as *Trust of Property Shares*, *Archimedes*, and *Jove* are all absent. But the list does include all those investment trusts which operate a savings scheme. So if you want to keep your dealing costs low by investing through a savings scheme, the AITC list is the best place to start your search.

Share price performance tells you how much you would have made if you had invested in the shares. The published figures don't tell you how good the managers were at managing the money. Nor do they give the size of the discount or premium of the share price to the net asset value. For this you need to subscribe to the AITC's monthly statistical service, which costs £2 a month.

USING A STOCKBROKER

Stockbrokers are also a useful source of information. The top stockbrokers for investment trust research, Warburg Securities, Barclays de Zoete Wedd and James Capel in London and NatWest

Wood Mackenzie in Edinburgh all produce performance figures. In fact, Warburg Securities and James Capel use the same figures which are produced independently for them and three other big City firms, Hoare Govett, Kitcat & Aitken and Phillips & Drew. But you won't have the right to receive these figures automatically, unless you are a substantial investor.

However, you may find that if your stockbrokers have access to performance figures they may be prepared to tell you informally over the telephone which investment trusts are, for example, standing at the highest discounts, or have the best net asset performance.

If you do want this sort of information you are better off trying one of the big stockbrokers with investment trust expertise, that is, if you don't mind paying their generally higher minimum commission charges. But remember, if you are only using their dealing service, they are likely to give you short shrift if you start abusing their good nature. There is a limit to how much free information these firms are prepared to give out.

THE AITC HANDBOOK

The best value handbook on investment trusts is produced each summer by the AITC. Called 'How to Make IT', it is published in co-operation with Woodhead-Faulkner and the 1987/88 edition costs £5.95. Each investment trust has an entry devoted to it, and follows the same format. You will find most of what you need to know about the individual investment trusts: their investment objectives, the size of the trust, the year it was registered, when the dividends are paid, any borrowings, any savings schemes, and where the money is invested, plus a five-year record of earnings, dividends, net asset values and share prices. The AITC publish an even more comprehensive yearbook, with a two page entry for each trust, but this costs £25.

If you have read this far you are no longer a beginner. But it is useful to know that the AITC also publishes a free introductory booklet called 'Explaining Investment Trusts' which explains the basics of investment trusts.

Of more interest is their free leaflet on savings schemes, 'Shares for Everyone', which tells you all you need to know about all the currently available savings schemes: how much you can invest regularly and as a lump sum and how much it will cost you in commission.

They also publish a free leaflet designed to help people choose a stockbroker; it is regularly updated, and they will send you a copy if you ask for it.

ASK THE MANAGEMENT

By this stage you may have narrowed your choice down to a handful of investment trusts. The management companies are normally only too happy to send potential investors a copy of their latest report and accounts and any recent reorganisation documents. Don't hesitate to ask for them – their names, addresses and telephone numbers can be found at the end of this book.

CONSULT THE FINANCIAL PRESS

Once you have taken the plunge and embarked on your career as an investment trust investor you need to keep track of your investment. The financial pages in the newspapers are the place to start. There was a time when there was hardly a mention of investment trusts at all. Now the sector is newsworthy, and investment trusts are generating quite a few column inches, especially when a particular investment trust is under threat from a predator. The Saturday family finance pages of the *Daily Telegraph*, the *Independent*, *The Times* ,*The Guardian* and the *Financial Times* all run features on investment trusts.

Money Observer publishes a quarterly magazine devoted to investment trusts. A subscription costs £10 a year from Investment Trusts Subscription Department, 120-126 Lavender Avenue, Mitcham, Surrey CR4 3HP.

You can check the share prices in your newspaper. Most give prices for the larger investment trusts. But you will need to consult the *Financial Times* if your taste runs to the more obscure investment trusts. The *Financial Times* shows the previous day's share price, the highest and lowest share price in the previous year, the net dividend in pence per share, and the yield shown as a percentage.

19 ENCOURAGING THE SMALL SAVER

If there is one thing that will get the investment trust message across, it is their savings schemes. The first was launched in 1984 by Foreign & Colonial, and now most of the big management companies, and some of the smaller ones, have one.

Investment trusts lost out in the battle for the small investor because so few people even knew they existed, and those that did were often put off by the fact that the shares had to be bought and sold through a stockbroker.

As public companies, investment trusts are prohibited from advertising their shares. However, the development of savings schemes has given the management companies the opportunity to start actively promoting the advantages of investment trusts for the first time. They have the further advantage of allowing the small investor to buy directly from the management company at very low levels of commission.

For years investment trusts suffered at a disadvantge to unit trusts. The advent of savings schemes means investment trusts are no longer battling with one hand tied behind their backs.

In fact the name 'savings scheme' is a little misleading. You can certainly save regular monthly amounts through an investment trust savings scheme. But you can also use the schemes for investing lump sums as well. Most investment trusts operate a minimum for lump sum investments of £250. Many unit trusts now impose much higher investment minimums, so if you only want to invest a small amount as a lump sum, investment trusts are often more welcoming than unit trusts.

This chapter is principally about how you can save regularly through investment trusts. However, the table of regular savings schemes at the end of the chapter also includes details of how to invest a lump sum as well.

REASONS FOR REGULAR SAVINGS

It is very easy to fritter money away. Most people find it very difficult to save, but are grateful when they are forced to.

Having a building society account and promising yourself that you will save something each month is not a good way to go about it. It's too easy to conveniently forget one month. Much better to set up a standing order to a savings account where you can't get hold of the money at the drop of a hat. This way you have to save, and most people say they never miss the money going out of their account each month.

There are any number of ways to save a regular amount each month. The one you choose depends on a number of factors, such as how soon you need the money, do you need an income from it, are you prepared to take a risk.

Unit trust and investment trust savings schemes are one of the best ways of saving for the long-term. But no one should consider taking out one of these savings schemes unless they are prepared to leave their savings to accumulate for at least five years – over any shorter period, the investor may not get the best return for his or her money. And you shouldn't think of taking out one of these schemes unless you have already an emergency fund which you can draw on fairly easily if your roof blows off, or your car blows up on the motorway.

Having said that, if you want a long-term savings plan you are likely to do better putting your money in a scheme linked to equities such as unit trusts and investment trusts rather than in National Savings, a bank or a building society.

POUND-COST AVERAGING

There is also the added advantage of pound-cost averaging. This is the phenomenon common to savings schemes where a fixed amount is invested each month into a fund whose price fluctuates. Pound-cost averaging has the effect of giving you more units or shares than would be the case if you invested in something with a fixed price.

For example, if you invest £100 a month in an investment trust savings scheme and in the first month the shares cost 100p, the next month 110p, and in the next month 90p, the average price of your shares is 100p, but instead of buying 300 shares, you have bought 302 shares. This is illustrated below.

How pound cost averaging works

	Monthly investment £	*Share price* p	*Number of shares bought*
Month 1	100	100	100.00
Month 2	100	110	90.90
Month 3	100	90	111.10
Total	300	300	302.00
Average monthly investment	100	100	100.67

It is one thing to understand the principle of pound-cost averaging, but it is quite another to be convinced of its merits. After all, our illustration shows prices fluctuating quite widely within a three-month period, which may not happen in practice, added to which the benefit itself doesn't look that significant. But as long as you think of a savings plan as a long-term investment, the benefits of pound-cost averaging are very definitely worth having. It also explains why, when you choose an investment trust savings plan, it is worth putting your money into an investment trust where the performance is likely to be volatile.

There are three ways of saving money regularly through investment trusts.

- Investment trust savings schemes;
- Life insurance and personal pension plan schemes;
- Personal Equity Plans (PEPs).

Investment trust regular savings schemes

All the big investment trust management companies and many of the small ones now offer regular savings schemes. The notable exceptions are Edinburgh Fund Managers, Gartmore, Henderson, MIM and Murray Johnstone. The minimum investment is usually just £25 a month. The commission you pay is remarkably low because you buy directly from the investment trust manager, who places a bulk order with a firm of stockbrokers.

If you don't want to take an income from your investment trust shares while you are saving, all the schemes will reinvest the dividend income in further shares. This facility is also available to any shareholder, whether they have bought their shares through a savings scheme or through a stockbroker.

Savings schemes have undoubtedly broadened the appeal of investment trusts, but nonetheless there are some limitations. So far you can only invest in investment trust ordinary shares. There are no savings schemes linked to split capital investment trusts, or the other forms of investments such as preference shares, convertibles or warrants. Hopefully, it is only a matter of time before someone launches a savings scheme linked at the very least to the capital shares of a split capital investment trust. Details of regular savings schemes are at the end of this chapter.

Life insurance schemes

A handful of life insurance companies run bond funds which invest in investment trust shares. Some of these funds are run in conjunction with investment management groups and only invest in that group's investment trusts. For example City of Edinburgh Life Assurance Company have two funds, one invested in 12 investment trusts managed by Ivory & Sime, another which invests in six investment trust and five unit trusts managed by Murray Johnstone. Other insurance companies have funds which invest in a range of investment trusts chosen from a number of management groups. You can find details of the schemes at the end of this chapter.

These bond funds are similiar to unit trusts in that the fund is divided into units whose price reflects the value of the fund's underlying investments. The difference is that in order to qualify for certain, and now fairly limited, tax advantages, you can only invest in them if you agree to take out a small amount of life insurance. You can invest a lump sum in a single premium policy, or save regular amounts in a regular premium policy which must be for a period of at least ten years.

People usually buy these policies because some insurance broker has managed to talk them into it. Many of these policy holders would be better off buying investment trust shares directly from the managers through a savings scheme.

There are one or two exceptions. There is no tax to pay on regular premium policies if you manage to keep them going for three-quarters of their term, which usually means for seven and a half years. The life insurance fund does pay tax, but as this is at a fairly modest level, higher rate taxpayers do enjoy a tax advantge.

You may be liable to higher rate tax when you cash in a single premium policy. But if you regularly use up your entire capital gains tax allowance, the eventual higher rate tax bill on bonds is often less than the capital gains tax you would pay on the profit you make on a direct investment in investment trusts.

Single premium insurance bonds are often recommended for higher rate taxpayers who expect to become basic rate taxpayers at some point in the future, say after retirement. The idea is you take out the bond while you still a higher rate taxpayer and cash it in tax free once you become a basic rate taxpayer.

Personal pension plan schemes

There is not much to be said in favour of investing in investment trusts via the vehicle of a single premium bond or a regular savings life insurance policy. Personal pensions on the other hand offer more tax advantages than any other method of saving. The amount of money you invest up to certain limits – normally 17.5 per cent of earnings – is tax deductble at your highest rate of tax. At the same time the insurance company is allowed to invest the money almost tax-free. If you are self-employed or your company doesn't have a company pension scheme, you should lose no time taking out a personal pension plan.

From July 1988, anyone in a company pension scheme has the right to leave it and make contributions into a personal pension scheme instead. This may be a good idea for younger employees who expect to change jobs often. Older employees – above 40 for women, 45 for men, should think very carefully before opting out of company pension schemes.

But if you do put money into a personal pension scheme the money isn't entirely locked away until you retire. Most building societies and banks allow you to use personal pension plans as security for mortgage loans, and most have loan-back arrangements which allow you to borrow money for other purposes as well.

If you fancy investing your pension contributions, or at least some of them, in investment trusts, several insurance companies offer pension funds which invest in a selection of investment trusts shares. You can find details of these schemes at the end of this chapter.

Personal Equity Plans

Personal Equity Plans, or PEPs as they are more commonly known, are investment schemes designed to encourage people to invest directly in UK quoted shares. If you keep a PEP going for at least one calendar year, there is no tax to pay when you sell. You can invest up to £3,000 each year.

Unfortunately, even though investment trusts are UK quoted companies, and should by rights be permitted investments for the purposes of PEPs, the government, when it introduced the scheme in the 1986 Finance Act, grouped them with unit trusts and put restrictions on their inclusion.

As things stand, if you go for a mixed PEP investing in shares, investment trusts and unit trusts, up to 25 per cent, or £750, can be invested in investment trusts or unit trusts. But if you go for a scheme which only offers investment trusts or unit trusts, you can only put in £540.

PEPs are costly to administer, and before you take out a scheme it is important to check that the management charges don't wipe out any tax advantage. It is this point which made most investment trust management groups reluctant to launch their own PEP schemes.

Alliance and Robert Fleming are the only two to have taken the plunge. The Alliance PEP is linked to their two investment trusts, *Alliance* and *Second Alliance*, so the amount you can invest is restricted to £540 a year. However, the charges are reasonable. Alliance charge the same as for their regular savings scheme, details of which are contained in the table at the end of this chapter.

The Robert Fleming scheme is run by Save & Prosper and you have the choice of a mixed scheme in which case you can invest up to £750 in investment trusts, or an investment trust scheme in which case you are restricted to £540 a year.

PEPs are a good idea for higher rate taxpayers who may be thinking of building up a portfolio of shares over the years through PEPs, or for seasoned investors who regularly use up their capital gains tax allowance, which stood at £5,000 in the 1988-89 tax year. For everyone else the tax advantages aren't sufficient to make PEPs a really attractive buy.

Life insurance funds investing in investment trusts

Insurance company	*Investment fund*	*Policies*
City of Edinburgh Life Assurance	1) Ivory & Sime Bond Fund. A fund invested in Ivory & Sime investment trusts	Single premium bond.
	2) Murray Johnstone Bond Fund. A fund invested in Murray Johnstone investment and unit trusts	Single premium bond.
Commercial Union Assurance	Commercial Union Investment Trust Fund. A fund invested in around 10 investment trusts	Single premium bond. 3 regular savings plans.
Continental Life Insurance	Continental Life Investment Trust Fund.	Single premium bond.
Crown Financial Management	Crown Life Investment Trust Fund. A fund of about 20 investment trusts	Single premium bond. 3 regular savings plans.
London and Manchester Assurance	London and Manchester Investment Trust Fund A fund investigating in about 80 trusts	Single premium bond. 4 regular savings plans.
Tunbridge Wells Equitable Friendly Society	1) Ivory & Sime Prize Plan Exempt Fund. A fund invested in Ivory & Sime investment trusts	Regular savings plan.
	2) beehive Bond Exempt Fund. A fund investing in a wide range of investment trusts	Regular savings plan.

REGULAR SAVINGS SCHEMES

Managers	Regular savings min. monthly £	Lump sum min £	Dividend re-investment
Alliance and Second Alliance (self-managed)	25	250	yes
BAILLIE GIFFORD BG Japan BG Shin Nippon BG Technology Mid Wynd Scottish Mortgage	30	250(1)	yes
DUNEDIN First Scottish American Dundee & London Edinburgh Investment Northern American	30	250	yes
FOREIGN & COLONIAL Foreign & Colonial F & C Alliance F & C Enterprise F & C Eurotrust F & C Pacific	25	250	yes
GLASGOW INVESTMENT MANAGERS Shires	20	250	yes
GLOBE GROUP Globe	25	250	yes
GT GT Japan	25	250	yes

Purchase	Selling facility	Commission	Other charges
monthly	yes	subject to competitive tender by brokers	purchase 50p, sale £5
weekly:lump sums monthly:regular savings	yes	0.2% purchase, min £12 sale	sale £10
daily:lump sums monthly:regular savings	yes	not exceeding 0.5%	nil
monthly	no special arrange- ment	on application	nil
monthly	no special arrange- ment	on application	nil
monthly	Yes:if shares held for 6 months.	0.2% purchase/sale	nil
monthly	no special arrange- ments	on application	nil

115

Managers	Regular savings min. monthly £	Lump sum min £	Dividend re-investment
HAMBROS BANK City of Oxford Hambros Investment	30	300	yes
IVORY & SIME Atlantic Assets British Assets Continental Assets First Charlotte Independent Investors Capital Japan Assets Pacific Assets Personal Assets Viking Resources	20	250	yes
KLEINWORT GRIEVESON	scheme available mid-1988		
JOHN GOVETT Govett Atlantic Govett Oriental Govett Strategic	scheme available mid-1988		
MARTIN CURRIE Martin Currie Pacific St Andrew Scottish Eastern Secs Trust of Scotland	20(2)	200	yes
MORGAN GRENFELL	30	300	yes
ROBERT FLEMING Fleming American Fleming Claverhouse Fleming Enterprise Fleming Far Eastern Fleming Fledgeling Fleming Japanese Fleming Mercantile Fleming Overseas Fleming Technology Fleming Universal	25	250(3)	yes

Purchase	Selling facility	Commission	Other charges
monthly	no special arrange-ment	on application	nil
Daily:lump sums monthly:regular savings	no special arrange-ments		
		not exceeding 0.5%	nil
twice weekly:lump sums monthly:regular savings	yes	nil,but see other charges	3% commission paid to intermediaries on lump sums
		nil,but see other charges	purchase:1%,min £1, max £25 sale:1%, min £10
monthly	yes	0.2%	nil
monthly	yes monthly		
		0.25% purchase only	nil

Managers	Regular savings min. monthly £	Lump sum min £	Dividend re-investment
Scottish Investment Trust(self-managed)	25	250	yes
STEWART IVORY Scottish American	25	250	yes
THROGMORTON Throgmorton	25	250	yes
TOUCHE, REMNANT Bankers TR Australia TR City of London TR Industrial and General TR Natural Resources TR North America TR Pacific TR Property TR Technology TR Trustees	25	250	yes

(1) £100 min subsequent contributions
(2) May be invested quarterly
(3) £25 min subsequent contributions

Purchase	Selling facility	Commission	Other charges
monthly	no special arrange-ment		
twice monthly	no special arrange-ment	0.2% purchase only	nil
monthly	yes	0.2% purchase/sale	nil
monthly	no special arrange-ment	0.2% purchase only	50p

Pension funds investing in investment trusts

Insurance company	*Investment fund*	*Policies*
Commercial Union Assurance	Prime Series Investment Trust Fund A fund invested in around 10 investment trusts	Personal pensions. Directors and executive plan.
Continental Life Insurance	Continental Life Pensions Investment Trust Fund.	AVC scheme.
Crown Financial Management	Crown Pensions Investment Trust Fund.	Personal pensions. Directors and executive plan.
London and Manchester Assurance	London and Manchester Exempt Investment Trust Fund. A fund invested in about 80 investment trusts	Personal pensions. Directors and executive plan.
Scottish Equitable Life Assurance	Trustlink. Pension scheme can be linked to Baillie Gifford Japan or Edinburgh Investment	Directors and executive plan.
Sun Life Assurance	Scottish American. Pensions linked directly to Scottish American	Personal pensions.

20 TAKEOVER MANIA

Takeovers, unitisations, mergers, and reconstructions are now a feature of everyday life in the investment trust world. For the last ten years or so, investment trust managers have had to do the job of managing investors' money with one eye on the lookout for any lurking predators. One leading stockbroker, Warburg Securities, even publishes an annual list of major share stakes to help investors identify the next takeover target.

The reason for this corporate activity is not hard to find. Once again the finger points to the investment trust discount. As we have already seen, most investment trust shares change hands at less than their net asset value. This difference between the share price and the net asset value is the discount. It is also the honey pot into which predators dip their spoon – and it's a pretty bottomless pot. Stockbrokers NatWest Wood Mackenzie reckon that, taking all investments trusts together, there is more than £13 million tied up in investment trust discounts waiting to be released.

Corporate activity comes in several forms, not all equally advantageous for private investors, who are sometimes left feeling they are the poor foot soldiers caught in the cross-fire.

INSTITUTIONAL TAKEOVERS

These takeovers are made generally for cash, for between 95 and 98 per cent of the value of the investment trust after all the costs of winding up the trust have been met. The institution – and it's usually a pension fund or insurance company – then liquidates the portfolio making a profit of between 5 and 2 per cent on the deal plus anything extra from any shares owned before the bid was launched.

It was the British Rail Pension Fund which pioneered institutional takeovers with a bid for *Standard Trust* in January 1977. The bid failed, but the idea had been kicked off and a whole spate of investment trusts fell in the ensuing onslaught. In the two years which followed ten trusts – including *Standard Trust* which finally fell to the Prudential – were taken over by city institutions.

Cash-only bids have the great disadvantage of creating a potential capital gains tax liability. Pension funds cannot offer a share alternative. Some have got round the capital gains tax problem by issuing loan notes, but this is a fixed interest investment which may not suit all investors. Insurance companies, so long as their shares are publicly quoted, can offer shares as an alternative to cash.

With one or two exceptions – most notably the National Coal Board Pension Fund's bid for *Drayton Premier* in 1985 – full-scale institutional bids are no longer favoured. The big City institutions now prefer working by stealth. They use their investment trust shares as a lever to exert pressure on the managements to come up with schemes for eliminating the discount.

DISGUISED RIGHTS ISSUES

This is where a commercial company takes over an investment trust in exchange for its own shares. The trust's investments are then sold and the company gets a cash injection which it can use in its business. This type of bid is known as a 'disguised rights issue' because the company is effectively raising fresh money by issuing new shares, which is what happens when a company makes a rights issue. If you are prepared to take the commercial company's shares, the bid is usually pitched slightly above the break-up value of the investment trust. There is usually a lower cash alternative. If you accept the company's shares there is no potenial capital gains tax to pay – the liability is rolled over until you sell the new shares you have acquired.

Disguised rights issues became all the rage following Electronic Rentals' bid for Robert Fleming's *London & Montrose Trust* in 1982. It used to be argued that it was only the small to medium sized general trusts with easily marketable investments which would ever find themselves on the receiving end of this type of bid. This has proved to be mistaken. Robert Maxwell's BPCC showed that it was possible to take over a large investment trust when they successfully bid for the £344 million *Philip Hill* trust, while oil exploration company Carless Capel & Leonard demonstrated that having a speciality is no defence when they bid for specialist energy investment trust *Winterbottom*.

This type of disguised rights issue has been criticised in the City because the commercial company's existing shareholders suffer a dilution of their earnings, and unlike a normal rights issue they don't get a chance to buy the new shares being issued. In addition the investment trust shareholders get shares in a company which they may not want to invest in. Nonetheless, the disguised rights issue is normally the route which gives investment trust shareholders the biggest initial pay-off.

UNITISATION AND PARTIAL UNITISATION

Unitisation is the practice by which an investment trust transforms itself into a unit trust. Unit trusts are open-ended funds and the price of units reflects the value of the underlying investments. There is no discount on units trust, so anyone exchanging their investment trust shares for units in a unit trust under one of these schemes is effectively eliminating the discount on their investment trust shares.

Unitisation has been around for a couple of decades. *Securities of America* was the first investment trust to unitise way back in 1968, and there have been a steady trickle of schemes ever since. Some like Touche Remnant's unitisation of *Cedar*, and Martin Currie's for *Scottish Ontario* gave both management groups their initial toe-hold in the unit trust market, which they have both subsequently gone on to develop.

Partial unitisation is a newer variation. Here investors are given the choice of opting for a unit trust and for continuing with a smaller investment trust. If you opt to exchange your investment trust shares for units in a unit trust there is no potential capital gains tax to pay until you come to sell your units.

From the investment trust manager's point of view unitisation is far from being the ideal solution. Hostile institutional investors generally take their units and cash them in, resulting in a big depletion of funds under management.

The same goes for partial unitisations, although such schemes do have the advantage that the investment trust is left with a rump of investors who have taken a positive decision to stay with it – the unwilling shareholders having taken their chance to get out at or near net asset value. It's one way of finding out how many friends you have. When *United States Debenture Corporation* partially unitised, the investment trust shrank to about a quarter of its former size.

Touche Remnant refined the partial unitisation idea with their scheme for *TR Pacific Basin*, where shareholders were offered the choice of shares in a new investment trust specialising in smaller Far Eastern stock markets or shares in a new open-ended offshore umbrella trust, with four subsidiary funds, or a combination of both.

COMPANY-INSPIRED RESTRUCTURING

Unitisation is not the only route available to investment trusts under threat from disgruntled investors. The simplest solution is to wind up the trust. A number of investment trusts, including most of the split capital trusts, have fixed dates on which they are to be wound up. The discount to net assets on these trusts narrows as the winding-up date approaches. However, any investment trust can seek shareholder approval for a winding-up at any time. The winding-up solution is not a popular method of eliminating the discount to net assets because shareholders can end up with a potential capital gains tax liability.

The split capital route

In recent years investment trust managers have favoured taking the split capital route, and a number of investment trusts have transformed themselves into split level investment trusts. Up until the stock market crash of October 1987, this appeared to be a successful way of eliminating the discount. But of the schemes which have been proposed since then, *General Consolidated* failed to deliver the desired effect when its package of new shares continued to trade at a

123

discount, albeit a reduced one, while *Drayton Japan*'s scheme was thrown out by shareholders. Management companies with disgruntled shareholders breathing down their necks are under intense pressure to reorganise, and the proposals are becoming ever more complicated, and difficult to assess. So much so that the shareholders they are meant to appease are giving them the thumbs-down. At the beginning of 1988, Ivory & Sime proposed an index fund, an off-shore open-ended umbrella fund, and a number of specialist investment trusts as a method of reorganising three of their investment trusts. But two schemes, those for *Japan Assets* and *Atlantic Assets*, were rejected by shareholders. Only the third, for *Edinburgh Investment*, got the go-ahead.

OVERSEAS INVESTORS

There are now distinct signs that overseas investors are waking up to the idea that there are rich pickings to be had from the discount. Perhaps it is surprising they have taken so long. It was the action of US arbitrageurs which forced *Drayton Japan* to come up with reconstruction proposals which they then rejected because there was no cash alternative.

Australian investors have a sizeable stake in *Australia Investment Trust*. And now that *Foreign & Colonial* and *Globe* both have their shares quoted on the Tokyo Stock Exchange, Japanese investors are now alerted to their virtues.

21 THE FUTURE

What does the future hold for investment trusts? For the men and women who currently manage them, the picture is one of continuing confusion, torn as they are between the need to appease an unwilling group of shareholders – pension funds and insurance companies – who no longer need investment trust shares and who want out at the highest possible price, and the understandable desire to hang on to their funds under management, their empires and their jobs.

Not that this uncertainty need trouble the private investor. Quite the reserve. If anything, this constant pressure from big institutional shareholders probably helps keep the investment managers on their toes. And any private investor shopping around for investment management should need little convincing that investment trusts offer remarkable value for money and overall, a more than creditable, and in many cases outstanding, investment performance.

From the private investor's point of view, the investment trust discount gives them the chance to buy assets and a stream of income on the cheap, while the ability of investment trusts to borrow money enhances performance in rising markets. Anyone who chooses one of the top performing investment trusts gets first class investment management very cheaply, while anyone who backs a loser may have the consolation prize of seeing it taken over.

If private investors can happily play the 'heads I win, tails you lose' game, they still have more than a passing interest in the fate of the companies which manage their money.

The investment trust managers appear to have all the cards stacked against them, but this isn't the first time they have faced adversity. And it probably won't be the last time their critics have found that they are made of sterner stuff than their gloomy predictions.

DEFENCE IS THE BEST METHOD OF ATTACK

A pattern of offensive and counter-offensive is now becoming firmly established. A wave of investment trust takeovers is followed by a period of management company inspired reorganisations. It happened in the early 1980's when Touche Remnant and Fleming converted many of their existing investment trusts into specialists. It is happening now, following the takeover of the £300 million *Philip Hill* trust and the realisation that mere size on its own is no defence from attack.

To succeed any management proposal must appease all those unwilling shareholders, and as recent events have shown, these shareholders are becoming increasingly critical and fickle. Sheer inventiveness is no longer enough. This band of bolshie shareholders wants to get out, as near to net asset value as possible, and in cash.

One popular option – converting into a split capital investment trust – is now becoming less popular. During 1986 and 1987 this was the most popular method employed by managers under pressure to eliminate the discount to net asset value, while retaining funds under management. But the failure of the *General Consolidated* scheme which opened at a discount to net assets of around 10 per cent when it resurfaced in its split capital form in March 1988, and the effect of the stock market crash of October 1987 on the capital shares of the *Scottish National*, the biggest of all the split capital reorganisations, has more or less put a brake on any new schemes.

For a time though, it was considered the best way of seeing off unwanted predators. One even saw successful well-managed investment trusts changing their entire investment policy to go split capital once they found themselves under attack. For example *Drayton Japan*, with an excellent track record, proposed to convert itself into a UK split capital investment trust when under pressure from a US arbitrageur. The fact that investment managers, MIM Britannia, only have a mediocre investment record in UK didn't deter them. The proposal, which included an interesting type of new income share, was rejected by shareholders because there was no exit for cash.

Ivory & Sime also failed to win shareholder approval to reorganise *Atlantic Assets* and *Japan Assets*. The schemes were judged to be needlessly complicated, even though a third scheme for *Edinburgh American* went through.

The message of the late 1980s is that the period of innovation which introduced stepped preference shares, zero-dividend preference shares, and deep discount income shares may now be over. Management companies must now come up with some new ideas, or they may have to accept the far from ideal – from their point of view – solution of unitisation or partial unitisations.

For the investment managers the big structural problem is the discount. But discounts will be with us for as long as there are more sellers than buyers for investment trust shares. The management companies may dream of shaking off the big City institutions and repelling the unwanted attentions of the asset strippers, but until they tackle the problem of the discount they will have to learn to live with the uncertainty.

The discount will only disappear when there are as many people who want to buy investment trusts as want to sell them. The management companies do have the power to effect a cure, but it's a bitter pill to swallow. To reach this state, investment trusts must either attract new investors, or they must accept a degree of contraction.

They get full marks for trying with their savings schemes which thanks to advertising are bringing the delights of investment trusts to a new generation of private investors.

But they are still being forced to compete with one hand tied behind their backs. Investment advisers and insurance brokers work on commision and rarely recommend investment trusts. All they can expect to earn, if they do, is the commission they split with a stockbroker which falls well below the commission of three per cent paid by unit trust companies and five per cent paid by insurance bond companies.

The Association of Investment Trust Companies (AITC) wants to see advisers paid on a fee basis rather than by commission. This is certainly happening at the top end of the market, and when in 1990 life insurance companies start declaring the size of their commission payments, the practice of charging a fee for advice is likely to become much more widespread to the undoubted advantage of investment trusts.

These are all very hopeful signs for the future of investment trusts, but until then they may have to accept that if they can't beat them, they might as well join them. For example, Scottish fund managers Martin Currie have found a way of paying financial advisers commission of three per cent on investments through their savings scheme.

And why have so few managers launched unit trusts which invest exclusively in investment trust shares? According to Opal Statistics this is big business for the unit trust managers with 10 unit trusts investing in investment trust shares with total funds under management of £441 million.

A recent fund of investment trust shares launched by Bristol insurance brokers Hargreaves Lansdown is another possibilty. This is a managed fund of investment trust shares with an initial charge of five per cent.

What is stopping investment trust management companies promoting their own investment trust unit trusts and working in conjunction with insurance brokers to form pooled funds of investment trust shares, along the lines pioneered by Hargreaves Lansdown?

But even if they did manage to attract large numbers of new investors, they might still have to accept a degree of contraction. It is hard for an investment trust to sign its own death warrant. Perhaps the best that can be hoped for is that one or two of the sleepier giants get taken over by an industrial company in a disguised right issue.

APPENDIX 1   SHARE PRICE PERFORMANCE AND TOTAL RETURN

To 31.12.87
Base 100

Trust name	Share price performance over:				Share price total return over:			
	1 year	3 years	5 years	10 years	1 year	3 years	5 years	10 years
ABINGWORTH	81.0	68.1	NDA	NDA	81.4	69.2	NDA	NDA
AILSA	107.0	156.8	237.9	NDA	108.6	166.0	263.9	NDA
ALBANY	110.0	146.7	293.3	573.9	112.8	159.9	342.3	874.8
ALLIANCE	82.0	121.3	187.1	323.2	84.2	132.0	215.2	454.8
ALVA	102.8	NDA	NDA	NDA	104.1	NDA	NDA	NDA
AMERICAN	72.0	87.3	135.5	228.9	73.6	93.4	152.6	306.7
ANGLO & OVERSEAS	86.5	129.1	216.3	346.0	87.9	136.3	240.0	465.1
ATLANTIC ASSETS	80.5	98.2	119.2	460.0	81.2	100.6	123.2	488.4
AUSTRALIA	88.7	NDA	NDA	NDA	91.5	NDA	NDA	NDA
BAILLIE GIFFORD JAPAN	96.4	129.3	350.5	NDA	96.4	129.8	352.5	NDA
BAILLIE GIFFORD SHIN NIPPON	98.4	NDA	NDA	NDA	98.7	NDA	NDA	NDA
BAILLIE GIFFORD TECHNOLOGY	106.3	81.0	NDA	NDA	106.5	83.6	NDA	NDA
BANKERS	87.6	141.2	237.6	421.1	89.4	152.0	271.5	619.8
BERRY	96.6	151.8	266.0	938.2	98.1	155.8	276.6	1,038.5
BERTRAMS	101.7	NDA	NDA	NDA	104.5	NDA	NDA	NDA
BIOTECHNOLOGY	53.6	76.3	NDA	NDA	53.8	77.3	NDA	NDA
BRITISH ASSETS	93.8	123.7	195.1	342.9	96.9	136.8	233.8	504.0
BRITISH EMPIRE SECS	94.7	137.9	NDA	NDA	96.2	144.6	NDA	NDA
BRITISH INVESTMENT	91.9	132.1	201.8	280.3	95.0	147.5	245.8	430.0
BRITISH KIDNEY PATIENT	108.8	172.9	185.0	NDA	112.1	187.1	205.6	NDA
BRUNNER	91.4	145.5	204.3	395.9	93.3	156.8	234.5	562.3
CDFC TRUST	NDA	NDA	NDA	NDA	NDA	NDA	NDA	NDA
CSC	124.2	144.4	203.0	292.9	129.2	166.6	268.4	542.3
CANDOVER	109.2	118.7	NDA	NDA	112.1	126.1	NDA	NDA

CAPITAL GEARING	155.1	295.2	703.8	5,228.6	155.3	297.0	713.1	5,353.9
CHILD HEALTH RESEARCH	102.4	148.3	296.6	NDA	102.4	148.3	296.6	NDA
CHINA & EASTERN	55.1	NDA	NDA	NDA	55.9	NDA	NDA	NDA
CITY OF OXFORD	114.0	175.7	273.1	515.9	116.9	191.4	322.3	794.6
CLYDESDALE	97.7	NDA	NDA	NDA	100.3	NDA	NDA	NDA
CONSOLIDATED VENTURE	117.9	173.7	208.9	289.5	118.0	175.5	215.2	327.1
CONTINENTAL & INDUSTRIAL	103.4	NDA	NDA	NDA	108.4	NDA	NDA	NDA
CONTINENTAL ASSETS	51.2	NDA	NDA	NDA	51.6	NDA	NDA	NDA
CRESCENT JAPAN	101.2	150.6	301.2	976.0	101.4	151.8	305.3	1,023.9
DRAYTON CONSOLIDATED	107.2	150.4	239.9	277.9	110.2	164.5	281.4	413.5
DRAYTON FAR EASTERN	96.1	156.0	267.1	650.0	96.6	159.2	277.7	759.7
DRAYTON JAPAN	105.3	187.0	336.4	533.3	105.4	188.6	347.7	696.1
DUNDEE & LONDON	109.7	144.2	193.5	377.8	112.5	156.9	223.3	563.3
EFM DRAGON	NDA	NDA	NDA	NDA	NDA	NDA	NDA	NDA
EDINBURGH AMERICAN ASSETS	72.3	88.8	108.0	334.0	72.7	90.1	110.7	360.9
EDINBURGH INVESTMENT	85.6	125.7	169.1	398.3	87.7	135.3	192.3	533.1
ELECTRA	110.8	152.2	250.0	500.0	113.4	164.9	291.9	757.8
ELECTRIC & GENERAL	83.5	138.9	266.9	529.9	84.0	143.5	283.8	642.5
ENGLISH & CALEDONIAN	NDA	NDA	NDA	NDA	NDA	NDA	NDA	NDA
ENGLISH & INTERNATIONAL	110.3	167.8	319.0	428.9	112.4	180.2	365.7	630.4
ENGLISH & SCOTTISH	92.4	138.6	265.8	531.5	93.5	145.1	288.7	684.0
ENSIGN	90.5	NDA	NDA	NDA	91.9	NDA	NDA	NDA
EUROPEAN ASSETS	50.2	88.5	NDA	NDA	50.7	91.2	NDA	NDA
EXTERNAL	94.7	143.2	217.5	466.2	97.5	155.6	249.9	637.1
F & C ALLIANCE	85.3	126.4	200.0	488.9	86.5	133.0	219.7	637.3
F & C ENTERPRISE	108.5	82.3	139.3	NDA	109.0	83.3	141.9	NDA
F & C EUROTRUST	47.9	123.3	250.8	370.0	48.6	127.7	269.3	451.3
F & C PACIFIC	82.1	127.9	232.8	403.6	82.8	133.4	257.7	544.7
FASHION & GENERAL	126.4	179.7	239.6	343.3	134.7	214.1	309.8	561.0
FIRST CHARLOTTE ASSETS	116.0	145.0	134.3	NDA	116.4	146.9	137.3	NDA
FIRST SCOTTISH AMERICAN	105.3	146.1	217.0	397.8	108.2	160.5	251.0	557.6
FIRST SPANISH	NDA	NDA	NDA	NDA	NDA	NDA	NDA	NDA
FLEDGELING JAPAN	111.9	104.8	NDA	NDA	111.9	104.8	NDA	NDA

To 31.12.87
Base 100

Trust name	Share price performance over:				Share price total return over:			
	1 year	3 years	5 years	10 years	1 year	3 years	5 years	10 years
FLEMING AMERICAN	64.5	83.8	112.0	215.0	65.1	86.4	119.9	285.0
FLEMING CLAVERHOUSE	102.0	174.5	275.2	500.0	104.5	191.9	328.4	778.0
FLEMING ENTERPRISE	116.8	160.7	280.6	470.0	118.8	173.9	329.6	712.4
FLEMING FAR EASTERN	89.4	137.3	256.3	500.0	89.9	140.8	268.4	651.5
FLEMING FLEDGELING	107.0	150.0	184.3	NDA	108.4	158.7	204.2	NDA
FLEMING JAPANESE	103.9	152.5	309.8	642.3	104.1	155.0	320.0	822.8
FLEMING MERCANTILE	90.2	141.8	219.7	400.0	91.9	153.0	251.4	565.1
FLEMING OVERSEAS	74.1	117.3	187.0	304.7	75.0	123.1	209.3	426.0
FLEMING TECHNOLOGY	84.0	90.7	138.8	292.5	84.2	94.0	149.0	365.8
FLEMING UNIVERSAL	77.4	126.8	208.1	324.3	78.2	133.7	233.3	442.3
FOREIGN & COLONIAL	82.6	139.5	253.5	470.6	83.7	146.8	279.6	605.0
GBC CAPITAL	79.2	86.0	NDA	NDA	80.2	89.1	NDA	NDA
GT JAPAN	90.7	136.8	266.1	1,082.5	91.2	140.0	277.6	1,253.8
GT VENTURE	NDA	NDA	NDA	NDA	NDA	NDA	NDA	NDA
GARTMORE AMERICAN SECS	72.5	95.6	192.9	332.9	73.2	99.2	209.5	442.8
GARTMORE EUROPEAN	62.8	93.5	166.7	401.6	63.2	95.5	172.2	439.2
GARTMORE INFORMATION & FIN	77.4	74.5	128.1	227.8	78.8	79.3	142.6	314.2
GENERAL CONSOLIDATED	105.8	149.8	251.1	425.6	109.4	167.6	305.5	678.6
GERMAN SECS	70.5	NDA	NDA	NDA	71.8	NDA	NDA	NDA
GERMAN SMALLER COMPANIES	48.7	NDA	NDA	NDA	49.0	NDA	NDA	NDA
GLOBE	96.9	147.1	245.1	326.1	99.6	164.0	298.4	501.1
GOVETT ATLANTIC	70.9	91.3	129.6	225.8	72.7	97.8	144.6	292.6
GOVETT ORIENTAL	76.6	140.4	253.2	449.4	77.2	145.5	272.6	571.1
GOVETT STRATEGIC	79.7	139.4	232.3	369.2	80.7	146.4	257.0	488.4
GRAHAMS RINTOUL	NDA	NDA	NDA	NDA	NDA	NDA	NDA	NDA
GREENFRIAR	75.6	159.2	294.2	820.0	75.9	162.1	304.2	919.9
GRESHAM HOUSE	137.1	154.5	207.3	944.4	138.5	162.3	227.3	1,200.7

GROUP DEVELOPMENT CAPITAL	110.3	NDA	NDA	NDA	110.3	NDA	NDA	NDA
HAMBROS ADVANCED TECHNOLOGY	NDA	NDA	NDA	NDA	NDA	NDA	NDA	NDA
HAMBROS INVESTMENT	86.0	129.6	184.0	404.4	88.2	139.9	211.3	562.1
INDEPENDENT	73.5	66.2	77.0	NDA	74.2	67.6	78.8	NDA
INVESTING IN SUCCESS	NDA	NDA	NDA	NDA	NDA	NDA	NDA	NDA
INVESTORS CAPITAL	109.5	NDA	NDA	NDA	113.6	NDA	NDA	NDA
JAPAN ASSETS	97.0	110.3	256.0	NDA	97.0	110.7	257.2	NDA
JERSEY GENERAL	126.9	168.7	227.9	342.7	130.6	185.5	269.9	518.8
JOS HOLDINGS	106.6	165.7	263.6	443.9	108.6	178.5	303.8	658.7
KEYSTONE	90.6	156.5	257.1	466.7	92.6	167.5	294.5	699.2
KLEINWORT CHARTER	96.4	141.3	228.0	385.5	98.4	152.1	263.0	560.9
KLEINWORT DEVELOPMENT FUND	134.4	NDA	NDA	NDA	137.7	NDA	NDA	NDA
KLEINWORT OVERSEAS	65.8	109.7	172.9	272.0	66.8	116.3	194.8	384.0
KLEINWORT SMALLER COMPANIES	146.8	242.0	369.9	606.7	149.7	263.3	436.1	925.8
LANCASHIRE & LONDON	114.1	145.3	216.3	465.0	118.1	164.0	258.4	682.8
LAW DEBENTURE CORP	93.5	147.3	253.1	486.0	95.8	160.4	296.2	734.9
LONDON AMERICAN VENTURES	77.2	NDA	NDA	NDA	78.0	NDA	NDA	NDA
LONDON & ST LAWRENCE	94.4	186.7	317.0	672.0	95.5	196.8	350.5	879.2
LONDON & STRATHCLYDE	100.5	117.5	229.3	458.5	102.1	123.3	249.3	598.8
LONDON ATLANTIC	117.2	170.1	233.3	395.2	120.0	187.8	279.9	608.7
LOWLAND	122.8	235.2	460.3	1,026.9	125.7	253.7	532.4	1,535.4
MAJEDIE	89.9	NDA	NDA	NDA	92.9	NDA	NDA	NDA
MARTIN CURRIE PACIFIC	85.4	NDA	NDA	NDA	85.5	NDA	NDA	NDA
MELDRUM	100.0	157.1	281.4	562.8	102.0	169.6	323.7	824.8
MELVILLE STREET INVESTMENTS	NDA	NDA	NDA	NDA	NDA	NDA	NDA	NDA
MERCHANTS	101.5	151.1	231.3	364.4	104.6	167.3	273.8	536.6
MID WYND INTERNATIONAL	77.6	102.5	276.7	NDA	78.5	106.4	297.9	NDA
MONKS	76.3	118.7	214.0	375.5	77.3	123.7	231.6	489.5
MOORGATE	128.4	203.4	301.7	654.2	131.7	228.1	369.8	1,011.3
MULTITRUST	NDA	NDA	NDA	NDA	NDA	NDA	NDA	NDA
MURRAY ELECTRONICS	84.0	49.4	NDA	NDA	84.3	49.9	NDA	NDA
MURRAY INCOME	98.8	151.4	267.0	506.3	102.1	169.0	326.7	746.3
MURRAY INTERNATIONAL	82.9	131.6	195.7	397.1	85.2	144.6	225.1	532.0

To 31.12.87
Base 100

Trust name	Share price performance over:				Share price total return over:			
	1 year	3 years	5 years	10 years	1 year	3 years	5 years	10 years
MURRAY SMALLER MARKETS	67.4	155.2	301.2	512.0	68.0	160.1	321.6	621.2
MURRAY TECHNOLOGY	89.0	56.5	61.9	NDA	89.5	57.4	63.5	NDA
MURRAY VENTURES	101.3	168.9	240.0	536.5	103.4	179.4	262.8	650.9
NEW DARIEN OIL	92.9	92.9	130.0	NDA	93.8	95.4	135.0	NDA
NEW TOKYO	93.5	110.5	268.7	NDA	93.6	111.5	271.1	NDA
NEWMARKET	50.0	31.2	25.7	NDA	50.0	31.2	25.9	NDA
NORDIC	71.6	NDA	NDA	NDA	71.8	NDA	NDA	NDA
NORTH BRITISH CANADIAN	132.0	184.9	248.4	578.2	134.5	201.0	291.9	832.2
NORTH OF SCOTLAND	89.1	NDA	NDA	NDA	89.8	NDA	NDA	NDA
NORTHERN AMERICAN	72.3	123.2	173.0	317.5	73.5	129.5	191.2	424.4
NORTHERN SECS	126.3	184.3	340.7	879.0	127.5	190.6	361.5	1,067.4
OCEANA DEVELOPMENT	127.9	NDA	NDA	NDA	127.9	NDA	NDA	NDA
OVERSEAS	74.7	100.0	156.1	302.2	75.6	103.4	165.7	383.2
PACIFIC ASSETS	85.1	NDA	NDA	NDA	85.6	NDA	NDA	NDA
PARIBAS FRENCH	NDA	NDA	NDA	NDA	NDA	NDA	NDA	NDA
PERSONAL ASSETS	104.9	130.3	NDA	NDA	105.8	133.3	NDA	NDA
PLANTATION	97.7	NDA	NDA	NDA	98.0	NDA	NDA	NDA
PRACTICAL	NDA	NDA	NDA	NDA	NDA	NDA	NDA	NDA
PRECIOUS METALS	128.8	188.0	175.7	NDA	129.0	190.0	179.5	NDA
PRIMADONA	NDA	NDA	NDA	NDA	NDA	NDA	NDA	NDA
RAEBURN	93.3	136.1	223.1	332.0	96.2	149.6	263.1	486.2
RENAISSANCE HOLDINGS	NDA	NDA	NDA	NDA	NDA	NDA	NDA	NDA
ROMNEY	69.2	113.7	182.8	297.8	70.0	119.3	201.0	397.2
ST ANDREW	98.1	160.3	236.0	390.8	100.0	171.8	267.1	550.7
SALTIRE INSURANCE	NDA	NDA	NDA	NDA	NDA	NDA	NDA	NDA
SAVE & PROSPER RET OF ASSETS	104.5	184.2	NDA	NDA	106.8	197.4	NDA	NDA
SCHRODER GLOBAL	76.7	116.3	152.7	310.9	78.3	125.9	172.2	420.7

SCOTTISH AMERICAN	92.0	150.2	206.5	372.1	93.3	161.5	234.2	498.7
SCOTTISH & MERCANTILE	108.2	145.2	246.5	NDA	113.9	167.6	299.5	NDA
SCOTTISH CITIES	117.8	146.4	223.6	341.7	123.1	169.1	280.8	546.5
SCOTTISH EASTERN	89.1	155.4	237.1	353.8	90.4	164.4	265.0	488.3
SCOTTISH INVESTMENT	84.5	139.7	216.4	364.6	86.2	148.2	240.9	488.5
SCOTTISH MORTGAGE	78.0	125.0	225.0	398.2	79.4	132.0	249.0	531.2
SECOND ALLIANCE	86.4	130.5	201.5	350.3	88.4	141.5	230.9	489.3
SECOND MARKET	55.7	88.7	NDA	NDA	55.8	89.8	NDA	NDA
SECS TRUST OF SCOTLAND	100.0	170.9	278.5	413.2	103.2	188.3	330.8	614.3
SHIRES	107.7	94.2	146.5	156.3	114.5	114.4	204.5	322.5
SMALLER COMPANIES INTER'AL	105.8	140.0	206.8	443.9	107.1	146.8	229.8	621.9
STRATA	65.1	NDA	NDA	NDA	65.1	NDA	NDA	NDA
STRATTON	93.0	NDA	NDA	NDA	93.0	NDA	NDA	NDA
SUMIT	127.5	NDA	NDA	NDA	129.1	NDA	NDA	NDA
TR AUSTRALIA	71.1	88.0	139.7	249.2	72.9	94.9	157.5	338.6
TR CITY OF LONDON	108.1	171.8	273.5	425.4	111.7	191.9	334.8	680.3
TR INDUSTRIAL & GENERAL	91.2	147.1	245.2	392.4	92.8	156.8	275.7	538.5
TR NATURAL RESOURCES	78.6	92.4	132.5	194.7	80.9	102.0	156.7	282.6
TR NORTH AMERICA	78.2	92.4	137.4	279.6	79.8	98.0	152.2	379.4
TR PACIFIC	NDA	NDA	NDA	NDA	NDA	NDA	NDA	NDA
TR PROPERTY	113.7	180.4	289.5	474.3	115.4	192.2	325.2	649.9
TR TECHNOLOGY	97.5	131.8	201.7	386.7	99.7	139.7	224.0	518.0
TR TRUSTEES CORP	112.2	168.3	271.8	464.2	114.2	179.1	308.8	658.5
TEMPLE BAR	114.8	170.2	281.2	415.0	118.3	189.8	346.9	688.0
THROGMORTON TRUST	121.3	183.0	283.2	531.5	124.1	199.6	335.3	844.5
THROGMORTON USM	113.7	NDA	NDA	NDA	115.3	NDA	NDA	NDA
TRIBUNE	93.3	141.7	268.4	478.1	95.0	150.4	298.5	613.1
TRUST OF PROPERTY SHARES	174.7	394.3	600.0	NDA	175.7	405.2	625.7	NDA
USDC	NDA	NDA	NDA	NDA	NDA	NDA	NDA	NDA
UPDOWN	123.7	168.3	289.8	569.1	125.8	177.8	317.9	710.3
VALUE & INCOME	109.5	NDA	NDA	NDA	112.1	NDA	NDA	NDA
VANTAGE SECS	132.7	289.8	546.2	1,092.3	134.9	308.3	621.4	1,522.5
VIKING RESOURCES	116.3	66.7	83.3	154.1	120.8	74.1	94.9	186.8

To 31.12.87 Base 100	Share price performance over:				Share price total return over:			
Trust name	1 year	3 years	5 years	10 years	1 year	3 years	5 years	10 years
WELSH INDUSTRIAL	204.5	NDA	NDA	NDA	204.5	NDA	NDA	NDA
WHITBREAD	114.2	155.7	173.4	467.1	117.3	171.5	205.6	679.7
WITAN	87.8	143.3	252.5	486.7	89.4	151.0	277.4	624.3
AVERAGE PERFORMANCE	90.1	133.5	213.7	389.3	91.8	142.7	241.8	538.1

Split capital trusts	1 year	3 years	5 years	10 years	1 year	3 years	5 years	10 years
AMBROSE	96.5	186.9	446.2	715.5	96.5	186.9	446.2	715.5
ARCHIMEDES	120.1	260.3	386.3	614.1	120.1	260.3	386.3	614.1
CAMBRIAN & GENERAL SECS	44.2	42.6	294.1	NDA	44.2	42.6	294.1	NDA
CHILDREN'S MEDICAL CHARITY	111.8	NDA	NDA	NDA	111.8	NDA	NDA	NDA
CITY & COMMERCIAL	90.7	164.5	312.1	822.7	90.7	164.5	312.1	822.7
DANAE	138.1	322.2	966.7	725.0	138.1	322.2	966.7	725.0
DERBY	109.8	178.2	250.0	545.5	109.8	178.2	250.0	545.5
ENGLISH NATIONAL – DEFERRED	118.2	236.5	406.0	705.6	121.6	260.2	481.2	1,034.0
EQUITY CONSORT – DEFERRED	110.7	162.4	224.6	621.4	113.1	176.5	260.9	898.3
FULCRUM	146.2	190.0	316.7	NDA	146.2	190.0	316.7	NDA
FUNDINVEST	95.2	158.2	295.9	630.4	95.2	158.2	295.9	630.4
JOVE	165.2	285.0	1,140.0	1,140.0	165.2	285.0	1,140.0	1,140.0
M & G DUAL	102.5	235.6	336.1	868.6	102.5	235.6	336.1	868.6
M & G SECOND DUAL	103.8	244.4	415.1	1,023.3	103.8	244.4	415.1	1,023.3
MARINE ADVENTURE SAILING	77.4	113.9	195.2	NDA	77.4	113.9	195.2	NDA
MEZZANINE CAP & INC 2001	82.4	NDA	NDA	NDA	82.4	NDA	NDA	NDA
NEW THROGMORTON (1983)	149.2	313.8	NDA	NDA	149.2	313.8	NDA	NDA
RIGHTS & ISSUES	111.1	161.9	NDA	NDA	113.0	170.0	NDA	NDA

RIVER & MERCANTILE GEARED	140.0	NDA	NDA	NDA	140.0	NDA	NDA	NDA
RIVER & MERCANTILE	NDA	NDA	NDA	NDA	NDA	NDA	NDA	NDA
RIVER PLATE & GENERAL	NDA	NDA	NDA	NDA	NDA	NDA	NDA	NDA
ST DAVID'S	90.7	NDA	NDA	NDA	90.7	NDA	NDA	NDA
SAVE & PROSPER LINKED	105.6	305.4	491.3	830.9	105.6	305.4	491.3	830.9
SCOTTISH NATIONAL	NDA	NDA	NDA	NDA	NDA	NDA	NDA	NDA
THROGMORTON DUAL	120.4	NDA	NDA	NDA	120.4	NDA	NDA	NDA
TOR	127.2	228.2	358.9	569.6	127.4	230.4	365.7	596.5
TRIPLEVEST	97.2	162.4	282.7	727.0	97.2	162.4	282.7	727.0
YEOMAN	103.4	NDA	NDA	NDA	103.4	NDA	NDA	NDA
AVERAGE PERFORMANCE	99.2	168.8	324.9	730.8	99.4	169.7	328.2	751.8

Source: AITC Statistics Service

APPENDIX 2   NET ASSET VALUE PERFORMANCE AND TOTAL RETURN

To 31.12.87
Base 100

Trust name	Net asset value performance over:				Net asset value total return over:			
	1 year	3 years	5 years	10 years	1 year	3 years	5 years	10 years
ABINGWORTH	102.3	86.9	NDA	NDA	102.6	88.0	NDA	NDA
AILSA	99.3	130.3	219.7	NDA	100.8	137.1	239.1	NDA
ALBANY	NDA	NDA	NDA	NDA	NDA	NDA	NDA	NDA
ALLIANCE	89.6	117.8	180.7	348.5	91.5	125.9	201.5	451.9
ALVA	100.5	NDA	NDA	NDA	101.5	NDA	NDA	NDA
AMERICAN	76.1	81.5	124.7	230.9	77.4	86.0	137.0	292.2
ANGLO & OVERSEAS	94.0	136.9	208.0	398.3	95.3	143.0	225.0	497.1
ATLANTIC ASSETS	74.9	85.4	108.8	390.1	75.3	86.9	111.5	409.4
AUSTRALIA	88.4	NDA	NDA	NDA	89.9	NDA	NDA	NDA
BAILLIE GIFFORD JAPAN	103.5	161.4	456.2	NDA	103.5	161.9	458.6	NDA
BAILLIE GIFFORD SHIN NIPPON	107.6	NDA	NDA	NDA	107.9	NDA	NDA	NDA
BAILLIE GIFFORD TECHNOLOGY	111.6	97.5	NDA	NDA	111.8	100.0	NDA	NDA
BANKERS	92.2	136.2	222.2	418.9	93.9	144.4	247.3	567.0
BERRY	97.1	148.5	253.3	760.2	98.2	151.5	261.5	825.9
BERTRAMS	NDA	NDA	NDA	NDA	NDA	NDA	NDA	NDA
BIOTECHNOLOGY	83.1	98.3	NDA	NDA	83.3	99.4	NDA	NDA
BRITISH ASSETS	95.2	127.7	202.5	368.5	97.6	138.4	233.2	502.3
BRITISH EMPIRE SECS	97.9	132.6	NDA	NDA	99.0	138.3	NDA	NDA
BRITISH INVESTMENT	94.2	125.9	185.6	317.9	96.5	136.8	214.4	437.2
BRITISH KIDNEY PATIENT	108.6	160.4	257.4	NDA	111.4	172.9	289.9	NDA
BRUNNER	94.6	139.7	197.2	399.7	96.5	148.4	219.8	518.7
CDFC TRUST	NDA	NDA	NDA	NDA	NDA	NDA	NDA	NDA
CSC	NDA	NDA	NDA	NDA	NDA	NDA	NDA	NDA
CANDOVER	128.2	192.3	NDA	NDA	131.3	206.8	NDA	NDA

CAPITAL GEARING	NDA	68.6	NDA	142.2	NDA	NDA	68.6	NDA
CHILD HEALTH RESEARCH	98.1	60.5	98.1	142.2	NDA	98.1	61.0	NDA
CHINA & EASTERN	NDA	113.9	NDA	NDA	NDA	NDA	116.2	NDA
CITY OF OXFORD	170.7	83.6	158.7	231.4	444.1	265.4	85.0	626.1
CLYDESDALE	NDA	124.1	NDA	NDA	NDA	NDA	124.2	NDA
CONSOLIDATED VENTURE	185.5	103.1	184.0	235.7	402.6	242.1		449.3
CONTINENTAL & INDUSTRIAL	NDA	61.5	NDA	NDA	NDA	NDA	107.3	NDA
CONTINENTAL ASSETS	NDA	103.9	NDA	NDA	NDA	NDA	62.2	NDA
CRESCENT JAPAN	183.4	106.2	182.7	372.8	1,030.2	376.8	104.0	1,074.6
DRAYTON CONSOLIDATED	145.4	98.7	136.0	204.5	281.1	229.8	108.1	369.9
DRAYTON FAR EASTERN	178.4	101.1	175.6	310.5	615.2	320.4	99.1	689.7
DRAYTON JAPAN	186.7	106.2	185.9	331.9	516.7	338.0	101.2	620.6
DUNDEE & LONDON	151.0		141.5	200.1	372.2	224.1	108.3	494.9
EFM DRAGON	NDA	82.3	NDA	NDA	NDA	NDA	NDA	NDA
EDINBURGH AMERICAN ASSETS	101.7	90.9	100.2	134.6	378.9	137.7	82.8	402.8
EDINBURGH INVESTMENT	140.5		133.0	194.1	449.7	213.6	92.3	565.4
ELECTRA	180.6	117.2	170.1	282.9	551.3	318.0	119.1	762.2
ELECTRIC & GENERAL	137.5	87.8	133.3	230.7	502.7	243.5	88.7	577.4
ENGLISH & CALEDONIAN	NDA	NDA	NDA	NDA	NDA	NDA	NDA	NDA
ENGLISH & INTERNATIONAL	172.7	110.8	163.0	279.8	428.8	312.0	112.6	569.9
ENGLISH & SCOTTISH	139.9	92.7	134.5	220.0	506.2	236.2	93.8	618.2
ENSIGN	NDA	96.2	NDA	NDA	NDA	NDA	97.1	NDA
EUROPEAN ASSETS	134.0	66.6	129.8	NDA	NDA	NDA	67.4	NDA
EXTERNAL	142.3	92.7	132.2	203.4	391.2	230.1	94.9	517.7
F & C ALLIANCE	134.8	95.3	129.4	192.9	456.0	207.7	96.4	556.2
F & C ENTERPRISE	105.5	107.6	104.4	157.1	NDA	159.6	107.9	NDA
F &.C EUROTRUST	158.6	69.2	154.1	250.6	318.7	265.8	69.8	374.6
F & C PACIFIC	150.3	89.1	145.5	224.9	434.4	243.7	89.7	544.2
FASHION & GENERAL	NDA	NDA	NDA	NDA	NDA	NDA	NDA	NDA
FIRST CHARLOTTE ASSETS	107.4	99.3	106.2	144.6	NDA	147.3	99.6	NDA
FIRST SCOTTISH AMERICAN	147.2	104.0	136.2	207.5	392.0	234.1	106.5	510.7
FIRST SPANISH	NDA	NDA	NDA	NDA	NDA	NDA	NDA	NDA
FLEDGELING JAPAN	131.2	118.3	131.2	NDA	NDA	NDA	118.3	NDA

To 31.12.87 Base 100	Net asset value performance over:				Net asset value total return over:			
Trust name	*1 year*	*3 years*	*5 years*	*10 years*	*1 year*	*3 years*	*5 years*	*10 years*
FLEMING AMERICAN	78.5	87.2	132.8	238.1	79.4	89.8	139.3	293.6
FLEMING CLAVERHOUSE	109.0	160.8	256.6	489.4	111.5	173.3	293.0	686.2
FLEMING ENTERPRISE	116.9	153.7	278.6	477.9	118.8	163.8	315.2	657.5
FLEMING FAR EASTERN	94.7	161.5	287.2	533.5	95.0	164.7	298.0	649.4
FLEMING FLEDGELING	106.4	147.5	194.8	555.5	107.6	153.8	210.7	695.0
FLEMING JAPANESE	110.1	186.0	355.0	690.9	110.2	188.5	365.9	833.4
FLEMING MERCANTILE	99.8	133.8	197.4	396.3	101.3	142.0	218.8	516.6
FLEMING OVERSEAS	83.7	121.8	192.7	339.2	84.6	127.1	208.8	432.6
FLEMING TECHNOLOGY	89.2	94.7	140.9	289.4	89.5	96.9	147.9	342.2
FLEMING UNIVERSAL	83.6	122.6	181.5	328.3	84.3	127.5	197.0	410.0
FOREIGN & COLONIAL	89.5	139.3	227.7	480.4	90.8	145.4	245.7	581.5
GBC CAPITAL	85.2	91.6	NDA	NDA	85.8	94.0	NDA	NDA
GT JAPAN	103.8	176.5	374.5	1,078.7	104.4	180.0	393.7	1,244.6
GT VENTURE	NDA	NDA	NDA	NDA	NDA	NDA	NDA	NDA
GARTMORE AMERICAN SECS	86.1	103.7	201.1	357.6	86.7	106.6	214.8	445.5
GARTMORE EUROPEAN	73.9	96.2	154.7	365.7	74.2	98.1	159.5	395.2
GARTMORE INFORMATION & FIN	86.4	80.5	127.8	234.9	87.9	84.8	139.2	297.5
GENERAL CONSOLIDATED	106.5	143.9	221.9	398.1	110.1	159.1	261.8	578.9
GERMAN SECS	85.2	NDA	NDA	NDA	86.4	NDA	NDA	NDA
GERMAN SMALLER COMPANIES	68.9	NDA	NDA	NDA	69.3	NDA	NDA	NDA
GLOBE	99.5	137.9	216.6	337.4	101.6	148.3	247.0	466.1
GOVETT ATLANTIC	78.5	89.9	125.5	229.1	80.0	94.8	136.6	277.7
GOVETT ORIENTAL	86.5	160.2	267.7	477.7	86.9	164.8	283.8	571.2
GOVETT STRATEGIC	76.2	126.0	191.1	346.9	76.9	130.9	205.9	424.2
GRAHAMS RINTOUL	NDA	NDA	NDA	NDA	NDA	NDA	NDA	NDA
GREENFRIAR	85.7	135.4	232.1	651.9	86.3	137.7	238.8	708.0
GRESHAM HOUSE	NDA	NDA	NDA	NDA	NDA	NDA	NDA	NDA

GROUP DEVELOPMENT CAPITAL	NDA	NDA	NDA	NDA	NDA	NDA	NDA	NDA
HAMBROS ADVANCED TECHNOLOGY	NDA	NDA	NDA	NDA	NDA	NDA	NDA	NDA
HAMBROS INVESTMENT	93.2	126.5	178.7	409.2	94.9	133.7	197.4	521.1
INDEPENDENT	68.8	70.7	86.4	NDA	69.3	71.8	88.0	NDA
'INVESTING IN SUCCESS'	NDA	NDA	NDA	NDA	NDA	NDA	NDA	NDA
INVESTORS CAPITAL	107.4	NDA	NDA	NDA	110.7	NDA	NDA	NDA
JAPAN ASSETS	96.4	121.1	281.6	NDA	96.5	121.4	282.7	NDA
JERSEY GENERAL	100.0	126.9	191.7	309.8	102.5	136.8	218.4	423.2
JOS HOLDINGS	107.9	162.6	239.8	439.3	109.7	173.6	271.5	608.6
KEYSTONE	93.5	143.9	232.6	451.2	94.8	151.4	257.7	609.5
KLEINWORT CHARTER	100.9	144.9	212.6	390.5	103.0	154.1	237.4	517.4
KLEINWORT DEVELOPMENT FUND	NDA	NDA	NDA	NDA	NDA	NDA	NDA	NDA
KLEINWORT OVERSEAS	76.9	121.2	169.7	291.8	78.1	127.3	186.3	377.7
KLEINWORT SMALLER COMPANIES	116.1	181.9	275.6	490.2	118.3	195.3	315.7	702.1
LANCASHIRE & LONDON	98.8	120.0	174.7	353.3	102.2	134.1	202.6	476.1
LAW DEBENTURE CORP	94.8	146.0	238.6	474.9	97.2	157.9	274.1	676.9
LONDON AMERICAN VENTURES	75.0	NDA	NDA	NDA	75.6	NDA	NDA	NDA
LONDON & ST LAWRENCE	95.0	158.6	323.6	NDA	96.1	165.7	350.9	NDA
LONDON & STRATHCLYDE	103.2	132.3	231.3	467.1	104.3	137.4	247.9	576.0
LONDON ATLANTIC	106.9	149.3	210.7	374.4	109.0	161.2	242.2	525.4
LOWLAND	104.2	183.8	338.7	745.3	106.3	197.6	386.7	1,041.3
MAJEDIE	88.6	NDA	NDA	NDA	90.4	NDA	NDA	NDA
MARTIN CURRIE PACIFIC	96.0	NDA	NDA	NDA	96.2	NDA	NDA	NDA
MELDRUM	100.3	146.3	246.9	496.4	102.5	156.5	277.0	669.2
MELVILLE STREET INVESTMENTS	NDA	NDA	NDA	NDA	NDA	NDA	NDA	NDA
MERCHANTS	101.5	140.6	197.6	366.9	104.1	152.7	226.0	495.2
MID WYND INTERNATIONAL	78.8	109.5	225.3	NDA	79.8	113.5	240.2	NDA
MONKS	85.5	122.5	200.3	381.2	86.3	126.5	212.8	463.7
MOORGATE	119.3	201.4	305.1	616.5	122.6	220.8	361.8	908.4
MULTITRUST	NDA	NDA	NDA	NDA	NDA	NDA	NDA	NDA
MURRAY ELECTRONICS	87.4	65.5	NDA	NDA	87.6	65.9	NDA	NDA
MURRAY INCOME	98.0	151.9	243.9	479.1	101.0	167.0	290.4	660.0
MURRAY INTERNATIONAL	87.6	124.2	185.7	386.1	90.0	134.2	209.1	486.9

To 31.12.87
Base 100

Trust name	Net asset value performance over:				Net asset value total return over:			
	1 year	*3 years*	*5 years*	*10 years*	*1 year*	*3 years*	*5 years*	*10 years*
MURRAY SMALLER MARKETS	74.6	148.0	239.5	461.9	75.2	152.1	252.9	536.9
MURRAY TECHNOLOGY	81.3	63.5	84.4	NDA	81.6	64.2	86.2	NDA
MURRAY VENTURES	110.2	167.6	242.2	526.3	111.9	176.1	260.9	616.7
NEW DARIEN OIL	85.2	72.9	97.3	NDA	86.0	74.6	100.1	NDA
NEW TOKYO	97.2	135.9	358.7	NDA	97.2	136.5	361.8	NDA
NEWMARKET	73.0	55.2	55.2	NDA	73.0	55.2	55.2	NDA
NORDIC	78.5	NDA	NDA	NDA	78.7	NDA	NDA	NDA
NORTH BRITISH CANADIAN	120.8	170.7	274.8	551.8	123.0	182.6	312.2	751.5
NORTH OF SCOTLAND	NDA	NDA	NDA	NDA	NDA	NDA	NDA	NDA
NORTHERN AMERICAN	81.5	123.7	180.3	350.9	82.5	128.6	194.6	435.7
NORTHERN SECS	119.5	164.6	268.8	662.0	120.6	169.4	282.3	767.8
OCEANA DEVELOPMENT	NDA	NDA	NDA	NDA	NDA	NDA	NDA	NDA
OVERSEAS	83.6	110.4	175.5	338.8	84.2	113.2	183.7	405.3
PACIFIC ASSETS	85.3	NDA	NDA	NDA	85.8	NDA	NDA	NDA
PARIBAS FRENCH	NDA	NDA	NDA	NDA	NDA	NDA	NDA	NDA
PERSONAL ASSETS	104.9	136.2	NDA	NDA	105.8	139.0	NDA	NDA
PLANTATION	98.6	NDA	NDA	NDA	98.8	NDA	NDA	NDA
PRACTICAL	NDA	NDA	NDA	NDA	NDA	NDA	NDA	NDA
PRECIOUS METALS	107.3	162.5	149.8	NDA	107.5	164.1	152.6	NDA
PRIMADONA	NDA	NDA	NDA	NDA	NDA	NDA	NDA	NDA
RAEBURN	94.3	121.2	177.0	313.3	97.3	131.6	202.2	418.2
RENAISSANCE HOLDINGS	NDA	NDA	NDA	NDA	NDA	NDA	NDA	NDA
ROMNEY	79.0	110.6	165.7	307.5	80.0	115.1	177.9	379.3
ST ANDREW	99.0	143.8	224.6	381.0	101.0	152.5	248.3	497.8
SALTIRE INSURANCE	NDA	NDA	NDA	NDA	NDA	NDA	NDA	NDA
SAVE & PROSPER RET OF ASSETS	115.8	204.9	NDA	NDA	117.5	214.2	NDA	NDA
SCHRODER GLOBAL	87.8	118.8	167.0	317.6	89.2	125.2	182.0	392.0

SCOTTISH AMERICAN	479.5	214.5	145.5	102.4	383.8	195.4	137.7	100.7
SCOTTISH & MERCANTILE	NDA	199.4	139.3	103.2	NDA	167.8	122.6	98.9
SCOTTISH CITIES	355.6	200.8	142.4	99.4	252.9	168.8	126.9	96.4
SCOTTISH EASTERN	453.9	223.7	145.1	91.0	356.4	205.2	138.7	90.0
SCOTTISH INVESTMENT	451.8	213.4	137.3	91.7	366.5	197.0	131.1	90.3
SCOTTISH MORTGAGE	527.0	228.2	130.9	84.6	426.1	211.7	125.6	83.6
SECOND ALLIANCE	463.3	204.4	128.1	92.3	360.7	184.0	120.2	90.5
SECOND MARKET	NDA	NDA	106.3	56.1	NDA	NDA	104.6	55.9
SECS TRUST OF SCOTLAND	566.5	270.4	165.8	100.8	422.0	238.3	153.7	98.5
SHIRES	287.5	209.0	139.3	107.5	146.1	149.7	114.9	101.7
SMALLER COMPANIES INTER'AL	549.6	227.7	135.5	103.1	423.6	209.4	130.3	102.0
STRATA	NDA	NDA	NDA	90.7	NDA	NDA	NDA	90.3
STRATTON	NDA	NDA	NDA	102.3	NDA	NDA	NDA	102.3
SUMIT	NDA	NDA	NDA	NDA	NDA	NDA	NDA	NDA
TR AUSTRALIA	282.1	145.4	88.2	74.3	224.9	132.3	83.3	73.3
TR CITY OF LONDON	585.9	281.7	171.0	110.6	404.6	240.1	156.0	107.6
TR INDUSTRIAL & GENERAL	455.4	218.4	129.3	90.9	361.4	200.2	123.3	89.7
TR NATURAL RESOURCES	237.4	118.3	91.7	84.3	182.2	104.8	85.3	82.6
TR NORTH AMERICA	315.7	138.2	91.7	82.2	251.6	127.3	87.5	81.0
TR PACIFIC	NDA	NDA	NDA	NDA	NDA	NDA	NDA	NDA
TR PROPERTY	519.1	272.7	168.7	110.3	409.8	248.5	160.4	109.0
TR TECHNOLOGY	428.2	184.5	118.8	90.8	349.1	172.0	114.4	89.8
TR TRUSTEES CORP	521.2	244.4	149.9	107.6	403.4	220.0	141.4	105.8
TEMPLE BAR	613.7	324.3	191.3	117.7	403.2	275.8	175.2	114.9
THROGMORTON TRUST	847.6	320.7	186.7	121.0	590.0	280.9	173.9	118.4
THROGMORTON USM	NDA	NDA	NDA	128.8	NDA	NDA	NDA	127.4
TRIBUNE	547.6	246.6	144.9	98.3	451.2	224.7	137.6	96.7
TRUST OF PROPERTY SHARES	NDA	NDA	NDA	NDA	NDA	NDA	NDA	NDA
USDC	NDA	NDA	NDA	NDA	NDA	NDA	NDA	NDA
UPDOWN	660.2	245.5	145.2	105.0	555.6	227.3	138.4	103.4
VALUE & INCOME	NDA	NDA	NDA	118.6	NDA	NDA	NDA	116.1
VANTAGE SECS	NDA	326.5	183.4	117.0	NDA	288.8	171.2	114.7
VIKING RESOURCES	150.7	69.9	56.8	103.7	129.8	63.5	52.6	100.7

To 31.12.87
Base 100

Trust name	Net asset value performance over:				Net asset value total return over:			
	1 year	*3 years*	*5 years*	*10 years*	*1 year*	*3 years*	*5 years*	*10 years*
WELSH INDUSTRIAL	NDA	NDA	NDA	NDA	NDA	NDA	NDA	NDA
WHITBREAD	112.0	164.5	181.5	551.3	114.5	177.8	208.7	758.8
WITAN	91.4	141.5	227.5	497.2	92.7	147.4	244.5	599.7
AVERAGE PERFORMANCE	93.6	131.3	202.4	393.2	95.0	138.2	222.3	502.4

Split capital trusts	Net asset value performance over:				Net asset value return over:			
	1 year	*3 years*	*5 years*	*10 years*	*1 year*	*3 years*	*5 years*	*10 years*
AMBROSE	109.8	164.4	283.7	390.4	109.8	164.4	283.7	390.4
ARCHIMEDES	NDA	NDA	NDA	NDA	NDA	NDA	NDA	NDA
CAMBRIAN & GENERAL SECS	NDA	NDA	NDA	NDA	NDA	NDA	NDA	NDA
CHILDREN'S MEDICAL CHARITY	NDA	NDA	NDA	NDA	NDA	NDA	NDA	NDA
CITY & COMMERCIAL	96.5	147.4	266.6	551.2	96.5	147.4	266.6	551.2
DANAE	NDA	NDA	NDA	NDA	NDA	NDA	NDA	NDA
DERBY	95.7	131.0	208.5	424.8	95.7	131.0	208.5	424.8
ENGLISH NATIONAL – DEFERRED	112.1	206.5	359.3	645.2	115.0	223.7	413.0	901.9
EQUITY CONSORT – DEFERRED	105.4	NDA	NDA	NDA	107.6	NDA	NDA	NDA
FULCRUM	NDA	NDA	NDA	NDA	NDA	NDA	NDA	NDA
FUNDINVEST	96.3	145.4	254.0	501.4	96.3	145.4	254.0	501.4
JOVE	NDA	NDA	NDA	NDA	NDA	NDA	NDA	NDA
M & G DUAL	111.5	183.7	316.5	615.8	111.5	183.7	316.5	615.8
M & G SECOND DUAL	NDA	NDA	NDA	NDA	NDA	NDA	NDA	NDA
MARINE ADVENTURE SAILING	68.7	103.9	150.7	NDA	68.7	103.9	150.7	NDA
MEZZANINE CAP & INC 2001	NDA	NDA	NDA	NDA	NDA	NDA	NDA	NDA
NEW THROGMORTON (1983)	122.6	242.8	NDA	NDA	122.6	242.8	NDA	NDA
RIGHTS & ISSUES	NDA	NDA	NDA	NDA	NDA	NDA	NDA	NDA
RIVER & MERCANTILE GEARED	120.5	NDA	NDA	NDA	120.5	NDA	NDA	NDA

	RIVER & MERCANTILE							
RIVER & MERCANTILE	NDA	NDA	NDA	NDA	NDA	NDA	NDA	NDA
RIVER PLATE & GENERAL	NDA	NDA	NDA	NDA	NDA	NDA	NDA	NDA
ST DAVID'S	NDA	NDA	NDA	NDA	NDA	NDA	NDA	NDA
SAVE & PROSPER LINKED	111.8	190.5	365.8	522.5	111.8	190.5	365.8	522.5
SCOTTISH NATIONAL	NDA	NDA	NDA	NDA	NDA	NDA	NDA	NDA
THROGMORTON DUAL	119.0	NDA	NDA	NDA	119.0	NDA	NDA	NDA
TOR	NDA	NDA	NDA	NDA	NDA	NDA	NDA	NDA
TRIPLEVEST	101.7	143.8	255.5	482.6	101.7	143.8	255.5	482.6
YEOMAN	112.1	NDA	NDA	NDA	112.1	NDA	NDA	NDA
AVERAGE PERFORMANCE	106.5	163.0	272.8	507.5	106.6	163.2	273.2	509.8

Source: AITC Statistics Service

143

APPENDIX 3 NET ASSET VALUE PERFORMANCE AND TOTAL RETURN BY MANAGEMENT GROUP

To 31.12.87
Base 100

Group name	Net asset value performance over:				Net asset value total return over:			
	1 year	3 years	5 years	7 years	1 year	3 years	5 years	7 years
BAILLIE GIFFORD & CO	86.0	126.1	217.5	298.9	86.9	130.7	232.3	336.8
BAILLIE GIFFORD JAPAN	103.5	161.4	456.2	NDA	103.5	161.9	458.6	NDA
BAILLIE GIFFORD SHIN NIPPON	107.6	NDA	NDA	NDA	107.9	NDA	NDA	NDA
BAILLIE GIFFORD TECHNOLOGY	111.6	97.5	NDA	NDA	111.8	100.0	NDA	NDA
MID WYND INTERNATIONAL	78.8	109.5	225.3	NDA	79.8	113.5	240.2	NDA
MONKS	85.5	122.5	200.3	271.5	86.3	126.5	212.8	302.3
SCOTTISH MORTGAGE	83.6	125.6	211.7	312.6	84.6	130.9	228.2	354.2
BARING INVESTMENT MANAGEMENT	97.4	137.6	224.7	309.8	98.8	144.9	244.6	351.8
STRATTON	102.3	NDA	NDA	NDA	102.3	NDA	NDA	NDA
TRIBUNE	96.7	137.6	224.7	309.8	98.3	144.9	244.6	351.8
CLAYTON ROBARD (UK)	81.4	NDA	NDA	NDA	82.8	NDA	NDA	NDA
AUSTRALIA	81.4	NDA	NDA	NDA	82.8	NDA	NDA	NDA
DUNEDIN FUND MANAGERS	91.8	132.4	194.1	277.2	93.4	140.1	214.1	323.3
DUNDEE & LONDON	106.2	141.5	200.1	288.0	108.3	151.0	224.1	344.6
EDINBURGH INVESTMENT	90.9	133.0	194.1	271.8	92.3	140.6	213.6	315.4
FIRST SCOTTISH AMERICAN	104.0	136.2	207.5	303.6	106.5	147.2	234.1	363.1
NORTHERN AMERICAN	81.5	123.7	180.3	263.3	82.5	128.6	194.6	300.3
EDINBURGH FUND MANAGERS	91.3	117.0	200.2	274.3	92.0	120.4	211.2	300.1
AMERICAN	76.1	81.5	124.7	156.5	77.4	86.0	137.0	182.0
CRESCENT JAPAN	103.9	182.7	372.8	656.8	104.0	183.4	376.8	669.0

EFM DRAGON	NDA	NDA	NDA	NDA	NDA	NDA	NDA	NDA
NEW TOKYO	533.1	361.8	136.5	97.2	528.5	358.7	135.9	97.2
SMALLER COMPANIES INTER'AL	349.0	227.7	135.5	103.1	298.2	209.4	130.3	102.0
ELECTRA MANAGEMENT SERVICES								
ELECTRA	NDA	NDA	NDA	NDA	NDA	NDA	NDA	NDA
ROBERT FLEMING INV MANAGEMENT	333.0	229.1	139.4	94.9	292.1	213.6	134.2	94.1
FLEMING AMERICAN	207.8	139.3	89.8	79.4	186.5	132.8	87.2	78.5
FLEMING CLAVERHOUSE	407.5	293.0	173.3	111.5	331.2	256.6	160.8	109.0
FLEMING ENTERPRISE	415.5	315.2	163.8	118.8	338.5	278.6	153.7	116.9
FLEMING FAR EASTERN	440.1	298.0	164.7	95.0	398.5	287.2	161.5	94.7
FLEMING FLEDGELING	354.8	210.7	153.8	107.6	311.3	194.8	147.5	106.4
FLEMING JAPANESE	547.0	365.9	188.5	110.2	500.1	355.0	186.0	110.1
FLEMING MERCANTILE	319.4	218.8	142.0	101.8	270.2	197.4	133.8	99.8
FLEMING OVERSEAS	290.1	208.8	121.1	84.6	252.5	192.7	121.8	83.7
FLEMING TECHNOLOGY	229.3	147.9	96.9	89.5	210.0	140.9	94.7	89.2
FLEMING UNIVERSAL	275.8	197.0	127.5	84.2	240.6	181.5	122.6	83.6
FOREIGN & COLONIAL MANAGEMENT	332.3	242.2	145.5	90.3	294.1	224.5	139.7	89.2
F & C ALLIANCE	306.6	207.7	134.8	96.4	272.3	192.9	129.4	95.3
F & C ENTERPRISE	NDA	NDA	NDA	NDA	NDA	NDA	NDA	NDA
F & C EUROTRUST	338.5	265.8	158.6	69.8	304.5	250.6	154.1	69.2
F & C PACIFIC	299.4	243.7	150.3	89.7	262.0	224.9	145.5	89.1
FOREIGN & COLONIAL	340.7	245.7	145.4	90.8	301.8	227.7	139.3	89.5
GM ASSET MANAGEMENT	439.3	324.3	191.3	117.7	336.9	275.8	175.2	114.9
TEMPLE BAR	439.3	324.3	191.3	117.7	336.9	275.8	175.2	114.9
GT MANAGEMENT	457.8	305.0	164.7	102.7	427.7	292.5	161.2	101.8
BERRY	381.5	261.5	151.5	98.2	363.0	253.3	148.5	97.1
GT JAPAN	675.9	393.7	180.0	104.4	623.1	374.5	176.5	103.8
NORDIC	NDA	NDA	NDA	73.1	NDA	NDA	NDA	78.5
NORTHERN SECS	371.8	282.3	169.4	120.6	341.7	268.8	164.6	119.5
USDC	NDA	NDA	NDA	NDA	NDA	NDA	NDA	NDA

To 31.12.87
Base 100

Group name	Net asset value performance over:				Net asset value total return over:			
	1 year	3 years	5 years	7 years	1 year	3 years	5 years	7 years
GARTMORE INV MANAGEMENT	92.5	118.1	197.5	254.5	93.8	123.5	213.9	290.6
ENGLISH & SCOTTISH	92.7	134.5	220.0	277.7	93.8	139.9	236.2	311.6
GARTMORE AMERICAN SECS	86.1	103.7	201.1	257.7	86.7	106.6	214.8	293.9
GARTMORE EUROPEAN	74.1	96.5	155.3	232.8	74.5	98.4	160.0	244.6
GARTMORE INFORMATION & FIN	86.4	80.5	127.8	172.1	87.9	84.8	139.2	198.0
LONDON & STRATHCLYDE	103.2	132.3	231.3	274.7	104.3	137.4	247.9	309.2
MELDRUM	100.4	146.5	247.2	313.1	102.4	156.3	276.6	375.2
GLASGOW INVESTMENT MANAGERS	101.7	114.9	149.7	147.4	107.5	139.3	209.0	239.9
SHIRES	101.7	114.9	149.7	147.4	107.5	139.3	209.0	239.9
GLOBE MANAGEMENT	99.5	137.9	216.6	265.6	101.6	148.3	247.0	328.3
GLOBE	99.5	137.9	216.6	265.6	101.6	148.3	247.0	328.3
JOHN GOVETT & CO	80.5	128.1	195.8	242.6	81.2	132.9	210.0	272.6
GOVETT ATLANTIC	78.5	89.9	125.5	147.9	79.9	94.8	136.5	167.4
GOVETT ORIENTAL	86.5	160.2	267.7	332.7	86.9	164.8	283.8	369.4
GOVETT STRATEGIC	76.2	126.0	191.1	244.4	76.9	130.9	205.9	277.1
HAMBRECHT & QUIST GROUP	75.0	NDA	NDA	NDA	75.6	NDA	NDA	NDA
LONDON AMERICAN VENTURES	75.0	NDA	NDA	NDA	75.6	NDA	NDA	NDA
HAMBRECHT/QUIST IVORY/SIME INDEPENDENT	NDA	NDA	NDA	NDA	NDA	NDA	NDA	NDA
HAMBROS BANK	95.0	129.3	183.1	245.1	96.8	136.9	203.1	287.5
CITY OF OXFORD	113.9	158.7	231.4	310.2	116.2	170.7	265.4	385.2
HAMBROS INVESTMENT	93.2	126.5	178.7	239.2	94.9	133.7	197.4	278.6
HENDERSON ADMINISTRATION	91.3	142.1	232.9	322.7	92.5	147.9	250.1	361.7

BRITISH KIDNEY PATIENT	108.6	160.4	257.4	NDA	111.4	172.9	289.9	NDA
ELECTRIC & GENERAL	87.8	133.3	230.7	305.7	88.7	137.5	243.5	332.9
GREENFRIAR	85.4	134.9	231.2	360.2	85.8	137.0	237.6	376.6
LOWLAND	104.2	183.8	338.7	524.6	106.3	197.6	386.7	651.2
STRATA	90.3	NDA	NDA	NDA	90.7	NDA	NDA	NDA
WITAN	91.4	141.5	227.5	313.9	92.7	147.4	244.5	352.1
HODGSON MARTIN	85.2	72.9	97.3	NDA	86.0	74.6	100.1	NDA
NEW DARIEN OIL	85.2	72.9	97.3	NDA	86.0	74.6	100.1	NDA
DAVID HUME INV MANAGEMENT	98.6	NDA	NDA	NDA	98.8	NDA	NDA	NDA
PLANTATION	98.6	NDA	NDA	NDA	98.8	NDA	NDA	NDA
INVESTORS IN INDUSTRY	112.7	158.2	235.2	302.3	114.8	170.1	268.9	374.1
LONDON ATLANTIC	106.9	149.3	210.7	275.6	109.0	161.2	242.2	344.0
NORTH BRITISH CANADIAN	120.8	170.7	274.8	343.7	123.0	182.6	312.2	420.7
IVORY & SIME	99.5	116.9	180.1	208.0	101.9	125.1	204.8	255.2
ATLANTIC ASSETS	NDA	NDA	NDA	NDA	NDA	NDA	NDA	NDA
BRITISH ASSETS	95.2	127.7	202.5	270.7	97.6	138.4	233.2	334.3
CONTINENTAL ASSETS	NDA	NDA	NDA	NDA	NDA	NDA	NDA	NDA
EDINBURGH AMERICAN ASSETS	NDA	NDA	NDA	NDA	NDA	NDA	NDA	NDA
FIRST CHARLOTTE ASSETS	99.3	106.2	144.6	NDA	99.6	107.4	147.3	NDA
INVESTORS CAPITAL	107.4	NDA	NDA	NDA	110.7	NDA	NDA	NDA
JAPAN ASSETS	96.4	121.1	281.6	NDA	96.5	121.4	282.7	NDA
PACIFIC ASSETS	85.3	NDA	NDA	NDA	85.8	NDA	NDA	NDA
PERSONAL ASSETS	104.9	136.2	NDA	NDA	105.8	139.0	NDA	NDA
VIKING RESOURCES	100.7	52.6	63.5	50.5	103.7	56.8	69.9	56.6
KLEINWORT BENSON DEV CAPITAL	NDA	NDA	NDA	NDA	NDA	NDA	NDA	NDA
KLEINWORT DEVELOPMENT FUND	NDA	NDA	NDA	NDA	NDA	NDA	NDA	NDA
KLEINWORT GRIEVESON INV MAN	94.2	138.2	196.5	266.0	96.2	147.6	220.6	317.9
BRUNNER	94.6	139.7	197.2	267.6	96.5	148.4	219.8	315.7
JOS HOLDINGS	107.9	162.6	239.8	326.7	109.7	173.6	271.5	399.7
KLEINWORT CHARTER	100.9	144.9	212.6	289.6	103.0	154.1	237.4	344.3

147

To 31.12.87 Base 100	Net asset value performance over:				Net asset value total return over:			
Group name	1 year	3 years	5 years	7 years	1 year	3 years	5 years	7 years
KLEINWORT OVERSEAS	76.9	121.2	169.7	232.4	78.1	127.3	186.3	271.0
KLEINWORT SMALLER COMPANIES	116.1	181.9	275.6	382.2	118.3	195.3	315.7	479.8
MERCHANTS	101.5	140.6	197.6	263.0	104.1	152.7	226.0	320.2
LAURWOOD	97.9	132.6	NDA	NDA	99.0	138.3	NDA	NDA
BRITISH EMPIRE SECS	97.9	132.6	NDA	NDA	99.0	138.3	NDA	NDA
LAZARD INVESTORS	87.0	116.4	171.9	235.6	89.1	124.1	191.3	277.2
RAEBURN	94.3	121.2	177.0	241.1	97.3	131.6	202.1	292.9
ROMNEY	79.0	110.6	165.7	228.6	80.0	115.1	177.9	257.4
LIECHTENSTEIN (UK)	85.2	NDA	NDA	NDA	86.4	NDA	NDA	NDA
GERMAN SECS	85.2	NDA	NDA	NDA	86.4	NDA	NDA	NDA
MIM	104.3	162.9	265.9	308.6	105.1	168.1	282.9	350.9
CONSOLIDATED VENTURE	124.1	184.0	235.7	348.5	124.2	185.5	242.1	370.5
DRAYTON CONSOLIDATED	106.2	136.0	204.5	229.1	108.1	145.4	229.8	275.6
DRAYTON FAR EASTERN	98.7	175.6	310.5	327.0	99.1	178.4	320.4	345.8
DRAYTON JAPAN	101.1	185.9	331.9	408.5	101.2	186.7	338.0	445.9
ENGLISH & INTERNATIONAL	110.8	163.0	279.8	309.9	112.6	172.7	312.0	371.5
MARTIN CURRIE INV MANAGEMENT	93.8	144.0	217.5	297.8	95.2	152.4	240.7	350.3
MARTIN CURRIE PACIFIC	96.0	NDA	NDA	NDA	96.2	NDA	NDA	NDA
ST ANDREW	99.0	143.9	224.7	303.7	100.8	152.3	248.0	355.7
SCOTTISH EASTERN	90.0	138.7	205.2	277.6	91.0	145.1	223.7	320.7
SECS TRUST OF SCOTLAND	98.5	153.7	238.5	335.7	100.8	165.8	270.4	407.4
MERCHANT NAVY INV MANAGEMENT	95.5	NDA	NDA	NDA	96.4	NDA	NDA	NDA
CLYDESDALE	83.6	NDA	NDA	NDA	85.0	NDA	NDA	NDA
ENSIGN	96.2	NDA	NDA	NDA	97.1	NDA	NDA	NDA

MERCURY ASSET MANAGEMENT	93.5	143.9	232.6	303.3	94.8	151.4	257.7	362.5
KEYSTONE	93.5	143.9	232.6	303.3	94.8	151.4	257.7	362.5
MORGAN GRENFELL & CO	91.6	130.4	200.4	278.6	92.8	135.7	215.3	314.6
ANGLO & OVERSEAS	94.0	136.9	208.0	290.9	95.3	143.0	225.0	331.0
OVERSEAS	83.6	110.4	175.5	239.1	84.2	113.2	183.7	262.0
MURRAY JOHNSTONE	90.1	139.8	214.9	301.4	92.3	150.2	242.5	357.7
MURRAY INCOME	98.0	151.9	243.9	322.6	101.0	167.0	290.4	414.2
MURRAY INTERNATIONAL	87.6	124.2	185.7	270.4	90.0	134.2	209.1	317.2
MURRAY SMALLER MARKETS	74.6	148.0	239.5	312.2	75.2	152.1	252.9	341.4
MURRAY VENTURES	110.2	167.6	242.2	373.7	111.9	176.1	260.9	415.4
PANFIDA MANAGERS	NDA	NDA	NDA	NDA	NDA	NDA	NDA	NDA
INVESTING IN SUCCESS	NDA	NDA	NDA	NDA	NDA	NDA	NDA	NDA
PARIBAS ASSET MANAGEMENT (UK)	NDA	NDA	NDA	NDA	NDA	NDA	NDA	NDA
PARIBAS FRENCH	NDA	NDA	NDA	NDA	NDA	NDA	NDA	NDA
J ROTHSCHILD INV MANAGEMENT	101.1	136.7	197.9	NDA	102.3	142.4	212.2	NDA
AILSA	99.3	130.3	219.7	NDA	100.8	137.1	239.1	NDA
PRECIOUS METALS	107.3	162.5	149.8	NDA	107.5	164.1	152.6	NDA
SCHRODER INV MANAGEMENT	87.8	118.8	167.0	228.1	89.2	125.2	182.0	259.5
SCHRODER GLOBAL	87.8	118.8	167.0	228.1	89.2	125.2	182.0	259.5
STEWART IVORY & CO	100.7	137.7	195.4	251.1	102.4	145.5	214.5	289.0
SCOTTISH AMERICAN	100.7	137.7	195.4	251.1	102.4	145.5	214.5	289.0
STEWART OLIM	116.1	NDA	NDA	NDA	118.6	NDA	NDA	NDA
VALUE & INCOME	116.1	NDA	NDA	NDA	118.6	NDA	NDA	NDA
TAI SECURITIES	NDA	NDA	NDA	NDA	NDA	NDA	NDA	NDA
CONTINENTAL & INDUSTRIAL	NDA	NDA	NDA	NDA	NDA	NDA	NDA	NDA
THORNTON MANAGEMENT	68.6	98.1	142.2	201.1	68.6	98.1	142.2	201.1
CHILD HEALTH RESEARCH	68.6	98.1	142.2	201.1	68.6	98.1	142.2	201.1

To 31.12.87
Base 100

Group name	Net asset value performance over:				Net asset value total return over:			
	1 year	*3 years*	*5 years*	*7 years*	*1 year*	*3 years*	*5 years*	*7 years*
THROGMORTON INV MANAGEMENT								
ALVA	NDA	NDA	NDA	NDA	NDA	NDA	NDA	NDA
THROGMORTON TRUST	NDA	NDA	NDA	NDA	NDA	NDA	NDA	NDA
THROGMORTON USM	NDA	NDA	NDA	NDA	NDA	NDA	NDA	NDA
TOUCHE, REMNANT & CO								
BANKERS	93.4	123.4	189.6	248.2	94.8	130.3	208.9	290.4
TR AUSTRALIA	92.2	136.2	222.2	323.9	93.9	144.4	247.3	389.6
TR CITY OF LONDON	71.3	81.0	128.6	159.3	72.3	85.7	141.4	184.3
TR INDUSTRIAL & GENERAL	107.6	156.0	240.1	318.5	110.6	171.0	281.7	406.2
TR NATURAL RESOURCES	89.7	123.3	200.2	248.4	90.9	129.3	218.4	286.7
TR NORTH AMERICA	82.6	85.3	104.8	134.6	84.3	91.7	118.3	161.1
TR PACIFIC	81.0	87.5	127.3	194.1	82.2	91.7	138.2	223.1
TR PROPERTY	109.0	160.4	248.5	293.0	110.3	168.7	272.7	339.4
TR TECHNOLOGY	89.8	114.4	172.0	247.2	90.8	118.8	184.5	279.2
TR TRUSTEES CORP	105.8	141.4	220.0	272.7	107.6	149.9	244.4	321.0
TOP TECHNOLOGY								
HAMBROS ADVANCED TECHNOLOGY	NDA	NDA	NDA	NDA	NDA	NDA	NDA	NDA
INDIVIDUAL COMPANIES								
ALLIANCE	92.2	125.4	189.6	275.3	94.1	134.2	212.5	328.2
SECOND ALLIANCE	89.6	117.8	180.7	286.8	91.5	125.9	201.5	339.3
	90.5	120.2	184.0	294.3	92.3	128.1	204.4	345.3
BRITISH INVESTMENT	94.2	125.9	185.6	257.8	96.5	136.8	214.4	320.8
CANDOVER	NDA	NDA	NDA	NDA	NDA	NDA	NDA	NDA
GENERAL CONSOLIDATED	106.5	143.9	221.9	298.9	110.1	159.1	261.8	381.9
MOORGATE	119.3	201.4	305.1	431.7	122.6	220.8	361.8	558.9

	Net asset value performance over:				Net asset value total return over:			
	1 year	*3 years*	*5 years*	*7 years*	*1 year*	*3 years*	*5 years*	*7 years*
JERSEY GENERAL	NDA	NDA	NDA	NDA	NDA	NDA	NDA	NDA
LAW DEBENTURE CORP	NDA	NDA	NDA	NDA	NDA	NDA	NDA	NDA
SCOTTISH INVESTMENT	90.3	131.1	197.0	260.2	91.7	137.3	213.4	296.0
TRUST OF PROPERTY SHARES	NDA	NDA	NDA	NDA	NDA	NDA	NDA	NDA
UPDOWN	NDA	NDA	NDA	NDA	NDA	NDA	NDA	NDA
AVERAGE PERFORMANCE	93.0	132.4	205.9	275.7	94.4	139.4	225.8	320.2
Split capital trusts								
GARTMORE INV (SCOTLAND) SCOTTISH NATIONAL	NDA	NDA	NDA	NDA	NDA	NDA	NDA	NDA
HENDERSON ADMINISTRATION	109.2	201.2	350.1	495.6	112.0	217.9	402.4	618.2
	109.2	201.2	350.1	495.6	112.0	217.9	402.4	618.2
JORDAN/ZALAZNICK ADVISORS MEZZANINE CAP & INC 2001	NDA	NDA	NDA	NDA	NDA	NDA	NDA	NDA
JUPITER TARBUTT RIVER PLATE & GENERAL	NDA	NDA	NDA	NDA	NDA	NDA	NDA	NDA
MIM	99.2	145.0	257.9	331.0	99.2	145.0	257.9	331.0
CITY & COMMERCIAL	96.5	147.4	266.6	359.6	96.5	147.4	266.6	359.6
FUNDINVEST	96.3	145.4	254.0	339.3	96.3	145.4	254.0	339.3
TRIPLEVEST	101.7	143.8	255.5	316.5	101.7	143.8	255.5	316.5
RIVER & MERCANTILE INV MAN	120.5	NDA	NDA	NDA	120.5	NDA	NDA	NDA
RIVER & MERCANTILE GEARED	120.5	NDA	NDA	NDA	120.5	NDA	NDA	NDA
RIVER & MERCANTILE	NDA	NDA	NDA	NDA	NDA	NDA	NDA	NDA

To 31.12.87
Base 100

Group name	Net asset value performance over:				Net asset value total return over:			
	1 year	*3 years*	*5 years*	*7 years*	*1 year*	*3 years*	*5 years*	*7 years*
NM ROTHSCHILD ASSET MANAGEMENT								
EQUITY CONSORT – DEFERRED	NDA	NDA	NDA	NDA	NDA	NDA	NDA	NDA
THORNTON MANAGEMENT	68.7	103.9	150.7	NDA	68.7	103.9	150.7	NDA
MARINE ADVENTURE SAILING	68.7	103.9	150.7	NDA	68.7	103.9	150.7	NDA
THROGMORTON INV MANAGEMENT	121.4	242.8	NDA	NDA	121.4	242.8	NDA	NDA
NEW THROGMORTON (1983)	122.6	242.8	NDA	NDA	122.6	242.8	NDA	NDA
THROGMORTON DUAL	119.0	NDA	NDA	NDA	119.0	NDA	NDA	NDA
YORK TRUST								
RIGHTS & ISSUES	NDA	NDA	NDA	NDA	NDA	NDA	NDA	NDA
INDIVIDUAL COMPANIES	112.1	NDA	NDA	NDA	112.1	NDA	NDA	NDA
YEOMAN	112.1	NDA	NDA	NDA	112.1	NDA	NDA	NDA
AVERAGE PERFORMANCE	105.9	159.1	257.6	333.5	105.9	159.4	258.5	335.3

Source: AITC Statistics Service

APPENDIX 4 TRUSTS LISTED BY AITC CATEGORY

AITC categories

A Capital and income growth: general
B Capital and income growth: UK
C Capital growth: general
D Capital growth: international
E Capital growth: North America
F Capital growth: Far East
G Capital growth: Japan

H Capital growth: commodity and energy
I Capital growth: technology
J Income growth
K Smaller companies
L Special features
M Split capital

Investment trust	AITC category	Net assets £m	Investment objective
Abingworth*	L	68.9	Capital growth by investing in fast-growing venture capital companies principally in high-technology and some special situations.
Albany*	A	9.0(1)	To invest in a wide range of quality stocks in the UK and abroad while maintaining a steady income growth.
Alliance	A	485.1	Steady growth of income and capital.
Alva	L	4.7(1)	To invest in unquoted companies which have a reasonable expectation of a flotation within the foreseeable future.
Ambrose*	M	29.4	Capital growth and maintenance and increase of dividends to meet the interests of both classes of shareholders by investing in marketable UK securities.
American	E	110.2	Long-term capital appreciation from investing in equities mainly in USA.
Anglo & Overseas	C	310.7	Long-term above-average returns mainly by investing in publicly-quoted companies with greater emphasis on capital appreciation than on income.
Archimedes*	M	5.6(1)	To invest in the capital shares of split level investment trusts to provide gearing for the capital shareholders, and high yielding equity shares to provide an increasing flow of income for the income shareholders.
Atlantic Assets	C	133.8	Long-term capital growth.
Australia	F	18.6	Capital growth in Pacific basin.
Baillie Gifford Japan	G	53.9	Long-term capital growth by investing in medium and small Japanese companies in emerging industries or with above average growth prospects.

153

Investment trust	AITC category	Net assets £m	Investment objective
Baillie Gifford Shin Nippon	G	14.9	Long-term growth by investing in smaller Japanese companies with good prospects quoted mainly on second section and over-the-counter markets.
Baillie Gifford Technology	I	10.5	Long-term capital growth by investing in listed and unlisted companies involved in specific high technology areas on a worldwide basis.
Bankers	A	143.0	To maximise total return (with emphasis on capital performance) by investing worldwide.
Berry Starquest	L	91.4	Long-term capital growth through investment in a selected list of quoted investments drawn from world equity markets.
Bertrams*	K	1.7(1)	Long-term capital growth by investing in small to medium-sized companies in the UK.
British Assets	J	401.8	Growth of income from a portfolio with an overseas emphasis.
British Empire	C	69.0	Capital growth from investing principally in undervalued asset situations.
British Investment	A	336.7	Long-term capital growth from an international spread of investments and a rate of dividend growth which at least matches the inflation rate.
British Kidney Patient	A	1.7	Capital appreciation and a gross yield of around 5.5 per cent a year.
Brunner	A	100.9	Capital growth consistent with income growth in excess of the rate of inflation from a portfolio with a significant overseas content.
CDFC	L	93.6	Long-term capital growth by investing in development capital opportunities outside the UK and Europe.
CSC*	B	2.5(1)	Capital and income growth by investing primarily in UK smaller companies.
Cambrian & General	A	131.9 (1)	Capital growth from a widely diversified selection of shares.
Candover	L	18.0(1)	Management buyouts of low and medium technology cash generating companies with capable managements and a good chance of profit growth.

Investment trust	AITC category	Net assets £m	Investment objective
Capital Gearing*	L	3.2	Capital growth by investing principally in investment trusts with some capital shares and warrants.
Child Health Research	D	1.6	Capital growth international without regard to particular geographical or sector distribution.
Children's Medical*	L	1.2(1)	Invested primarily in UK equities, but with 40 per cent currently in UK Government stocks, to produce income equivalent to FT-Actuaries All Share Index. Income paid to a medical charity.
City & Commercial	M	46.5	Invested principally in UK investment trusts and internationally based closed-end funds.
City of Oxford	B	16.2	Capital growth with steadily rising income.
China & Eastern	F	40.4	Long-term capital growth by investing primarily in companies with direct business involvement in China.
Clydesdale	C	12.2	Capital growth by investing primarily in UK stocks, including undermanaged and strategically situated companies which will benefit from positive management.
Consolidated Venture	L	29.2	Predominantly invested in unquoted companies which are within 3 to 4 years of a public quotation principally in North America.
Continental & Industrial	A	155.2	Above average returns through investing in a small number of high-quality international financial services businesses.
Continental Assets	K	10.2	Long-term capital growth through investing in smaller continental European companies.
Crescent Japan	G	105.8	Long-term capital appreciation by investing in Japanese equities.
Danae	M	6.7	Capital and income growth by investing in securities with an above-average yield, currently with about 50 per cent in fixed interest investments.
Derby	M	40.6	Balance of capital and income growth to meet the needs of both classes of shareholders by investing predominantly in UK quoted companies.

Investment trust	AITC category	Net assets £m	Investment objective
Drayton Consolidated	L	197.2	Investment in unlisted and special situations to principally increase capital with dividend growth as a secondary objective.
Drayton Far Eastern	F	44.4	Capital appreciation by investing in far eastern and Pacific stock markets.
Drayton Japan	G	239.3	Investment principally in Japanese equities.
Dundee & London	K	51.5	Flexible investment policy aiming for capital and revenue growth with the emphasis on smaller companies.
EFM Dragon	F	5.4	Capital growth by investing in equities in countries of Pacific basin other than Australia and Japan.
Edinburgh Investment	A	594.6	Long-term capital and income growth from an international spread of equity investments.
Electra	L	370.3	Unlisted investments and special situations.
Electric & General	C	90.5	Capital growth and steady increase in the dividends from investing on a worldwide basis in medium-sized companies with above average growth prospects.
English & Caledonian*	L	10.1	Capital growth by providing venture capital funds to UK companies with potential to obtain a market quotation.
English & International	K	63.6	More than 50 per cent invested in UK equities with the emphasis on smaller companies.
English & Scottish	D	96.1	Capital growth by investing on a worldwide basis.
English National	M	8.8	An above-average level of dividend increase by investment in UK smaller and medium sized companies but with substantial direct investment in property.
Ensign	L	278.0	Capital and income growth by concentrating on financial services companies and development capital investments.
Equity Consort	M	31.2	Invested mainly in UK equities including smaller companies.

156

Investment trust	AITC cate-gory	Net assets £m	Investment objective
External*	D	44.5	First objective capital growth by investing predominantly overseas but with a higher than average yield. Secondary objective to provide a rising dividend stream.
F & C Enterprise	L	31.3	To provide investors with an interest in young and emerging companies.
F & C Eurotrust	D	35.6	Equity investment in Europe, mainly in the Community.
F & C Pacific	F	174.8	Long-term asset growth by investing in the countries round the Pacific Ocean.
F & C Smaller Companies	K	87.1	Maximise total return by investing in an international growth portfolio of mainly small and medium-sized companies.
Fashion & General	C	5.7	Capital growth.
First Charlotte	K	10.2	Capital growth with emphasis on USM stocks.
First Scottish American	J	161.2	Growth of income without neglecting capital performance by investing in mainly UK companies.
First Spanish*	D	23.2	Long-term capital growth by investing in Spanish equities.
Fleming American	E	108.4	Best possible return over the medium term by specialising in North American investments with growth potential.
Fleming Claverhouse	B	51.3	Invested exclusively in the UK in companies offering capital and income growth.
Fleming Enterprise	L	55.5	Invested in small UK-listed companies and those not yet listed on a stock exchange.
Fleming Far Eastern	F	299.4	Invested in far eastern stocks.
Fleming Fledgeling	K	26.0	Capital growth from small companies in the UK and the USA.
Fleming Japanese	G	175.8	Invested in Japanese securities with emphasis on capital performance.
Fleming Mercantile	L	309.3	A wide geographical spread with an emphasis on smaller emerging growth companies both quoted and unquoted.
Fleming Overseas	D	237.7	Up to 90 per cent invested in international markets.

Investment trust	AITC category	Net assets £m	Investment objective
Fleming Technology	I	77.9	Investment geared to technology.
Fleming Universal	D	104.6	Invested in a well-diversified portfolio both by territory and industry.
Foreign & Colonial	A	800.2	Long-term growth of assets and dividends to keep pace with inflation.
Fulcrum*	M	3.5	To create a balanced portfolio providing a high initial income, satisfactory growth in that income and capital growth by investing in a wide range of equities and fixed interest securities mainly in the UK.
Fundinvest	M	36.8	Capital growth and income mainly by investing in UK investment trusts.
GT Japan	G	97.1	Invested mainly in Japanese securities with a view to growth.
GT Venture	L	11.6	Capital growth by investing in unquoted investments.
Gartmore American	E	30.2	Capital growth from investment concentrated in North America, with other investments not normally accounting for more than 40 per cent of the portfolio.
Gartmore European	D	17.1	Capital growth by investing in Europe.
Gartmore Information & Finance	D	49.8	Concentrating on companies substantially involved in financial and information services.
General Consolidated	M	78.3	Long-term capital appreciation and above-average dividend growth using a flexible non-specialist approach.
German Securities	D	8.4	Capital growth by investing in major German companies
German Smaller Companies*	D	20.8(1)	Long-term capital growth by investing in small and medium sized West German companies.
Globe	A	1,017.0	Capital appreciation above the FT-Actuaries All Share Index and dividend increases at least in line with inflation.
Govett Atlantic	E	116.0	Capital growth mainly by investing in North America.
Govett Oriental	F	325.3	Growth of capital and income by investing in the far east.

Investment trust	AITC category	Net assets £m	Investment objective
Govett Strategic	A	435.7	Growth of capital and income by investing in leading world markets and switching resources as prospects change.
Grahams Rintoul	K	35.2	Long-term capital growth by investing in UK companies capitalised at £150 million or less, with up to 20 per cent in unquoted securities.
Greenfriar	C	29.4	Maximum capital growth with less emphasis on the dividend beyond maintaining it.
Gresham House*	L	29.7(1)	To specialise in unquoted stocks including start-ups and private companies with a view to seeing them through to flotation.
Group Development Capital*	L	7.9	Capital growth by investing in development capital opportunities, mainly unlisted companies.
Hambros Advanced Technology	I	32.1	Capital growth by investing in high-technology venture capital opportunities.
Hambros	D	155.3	Growth of assets and dividends by investing internationally in listed and unlisted companies.
Independent	I	58.7	Long-term capital growth through investment in technology sector.
'Investing in Success'	L	51.4	To invest in companies which show outstanding growth potential.
Investors Capital	J	231.3	To invest in equities of companies with outstanding profits and dividends.
Japan Assets	G	95.5	Capital growth by investing mainly in small and medium sized Japanese companies.
Jersey General	A	54.9(1)	Steady growth of income and capital from a wide and flexible spread of investments.
Jos Holdings	A	12.8	Maximum possible income consistent with reasonable capital growth from an international portfolio with a proportion of special situations especially those with recovery prospects.
Jove*	M	17.5	Income and capital growth from a portfolio of high-yielding investments, currently with about 15 per cent in fixed interest investments.

Investment trust	AITC category	Net assets £m	Investment objective
Keystone	A	55.9	Long-term growth of capital and income through a balanced portfolio of British and international companies.
Kleinwort Charter	A	130.4	Income and capital growth from a concentrated portfolio which makes use of the possibilities of investment trust status, such as gearing and currency management.
Kleinwort Development	L	15.6	Capital growth by investing in unquoted companies which have attractive growth prospects.
Kleinwort Overseas	D	112.8	The content of the portfolio will normally be predominantly committed to foreign markets.
Kleinwort Smaller Companies	K	23.2	Principally invested in small UK companies.
Lancashire & London	C	8.2	Capital growth.
Law Debenture Corporation	A	70.8	Long-term capital growth and steadily rising income from a widely spread portfolio both geographically and by industry.
London American Ventures	L	62.5	Capital growth by investing in US venture market.
London & St Lawrence*	L	18.6	Capital growth and continuing growth of income by investing in investment trusts held by the Practical Investment Fund and the Practical Investment Co. (1941).
London & Strathclyde	K	37.5	Long-term capital and income growth by investing on a worldwide basis while concentrating on smaller companies and emerging industries. Investment in unlisted securities is a feature of the trust.
London Atlantic	K	33.9	Balanced income and capital growth by investing in small and medium-sized companies in the UK and overseas.
Lowland	J	41.4	Above average income return with growth of income and capital over the medium to long term.
M & G Dual*	M	80.0	Fully invested in units of M & G General, an M & G unit trust.
M & G Second Dual*	M	38.6(1)	Fully invested in units of M & G Dividend, an M & G unit trust.
Majedie*	A	—	To maximise long-term returns by investing in listed securities in the UK and overseas and in property in the UK.

Investment trust	AITC category	Net assets £m	Investment objective
Marine Adventure Sailing	M	1.6	Even-handed management between ordinary shareholders and loan noteholders throughout the life of the company.
Martin Currie Pacific	F	23.5	Long-term capital growth by investing in the fastest growing countries in the Pacific area.
Meldrum	A	57.8	Capital growth and an increasing dividend flow by investing in quality equity shares.
Melville Street*	L	22.9(1)	Medium-term capital growth by investing in unquoted companies.
Merchants	J	193.7	Above average level of income and income growth together with long-term growth of capital by maintaining a diversified worldwide portfolio in which recovery situations and the use of gearing will be given special emphasis.
Mezzanine Capital & Income 2001*	M	30.2(1)	To provide a substantial yield and significant capital appreciation by investing in LBOs principally in the United States.
Mid Wynd	D	9.5	Invested principally in smaller and less well-known growth companies traded on overseas stock markets.
Monks	D	213.4	Capital appreciation at the short-term expensive of earnings and dividends if necessary.
Moorgate	K	28.5	Invested predominantly in smaller companies and to a lesser extent in larger companies which may be due for a re-rating or to be taken over.
Multitrust*	A	1.7(1)	Long-term capital growth with regular and increasing dividends by investing principally but not exclusively in UK smaller companies.
Murray Electronics*	I	19.5	Capital growth by investing in unlisted electronic companies which have good prospects of becoming quoted without further capital injections.
Murray Income	J	193.7	High income return consistent with security and growth of capital.
Murray International	J	254.6	Growth in net asset value and a steadily rising income through an international portfolio.
Murray Smaller Markets	D	100.3	Growth in net asset value through an international portfolio with emphasis on smaller markets.

161

Investment trust	AITC cate-gory	Net assets £m	Investment objective
Murray Technology*	I	14.7	Long-term capital growth by investing in listed and unlisted high technology companies throughout the world.
Murray Ventures	L	65.6	Capital and income growth by investing substantially in unlisted securities.
New Darien Oil	H	6.0	Capital growth by investing in companies involved in all aspects of energy, mostly oil and gas.
New Tokyo	G	69.0	Long-term capital growth by investing in small to medium sized Japanese companies.
New Throgmorton (1983)	M	58.8	Specialising primarily in recovery investments to maximise interest and return to both capital and income shareholders.
Nordic	D	8.3	Long-term capital growth by investing substantially in Scandinavian companies.
North British Canadian	K	27.0	Capital and income growth by investing mainly in UK smaller companies.
Northern American	D	158.2	Long-term capital growth by investing in a portfolio of shares normally not more than 20 per cent of which is invested in the UK.
North of Scotland*	L	4.1(1)	Capital growth by investing principally in unlisted investments in Scotland.
Overseas	D	74.7	To invest solely in overseas markets with priority given to capital growth rather than income.
Oceana*	D	18.6(1)	Capital growth by investing globally.
Pacific Assets	F	16.9	Long-term capital growth by investing in Asian Pacific region, excluding Japan and Australia.
Paribas French	D	9.7	Capital growth by investing in French traded companies, including opportunities provided by French privatisation programme. The trust has an intended life of ten years.
Practical*	L	20.2(1)	Long-term capital growth primarily by investing in investment trust shares, both conventional and split level.
Personal Assets	C	7.9	Long-term capital growth specifically for personal investors.
Plantation	H	13.5	Long-term capital growth by investing in listed and unlisted securities in the plantation sector.

Investment trust	AITC cate-gory	Net assets £m	Investment objective
Precious Metals	H	23.2	Long-term capital appreciation through precious and strategic metal-related investments outside South Africa.
Primadona	D	5.9	Capital growth by investing in a wide geographic spread of listed investments.
Raeburn	J	134.8	High yield and above-average dividend growth.
Rights & Issues	M	6.4	Capital and income growth for both classes of shareholders by concentrating mainly on small to medium-sized UK companies.
River & Mercantile	M	104.0	Steadily growing income and capital by investing in larger companies worldwide with prudent management of currency exposures. The portfolio is presently invested mainly in the UK.
River & Mercantile American*	M	14.5(1)	Invested in US quoted securities, to provide the potential for capital appreciation with a high initial yield.
River & Mercantile Geared	M	17.0	To provide a substantial and growing yield with potential for significant capital appreciation to meet the requirements of the holders of both classes of shares.
River Plate & General	M	74.4	To aim for a good quality high-yielding portfolio bearing in mind the requirements of both income and capital shareholders.
Romney	D	101.7	To invest on a global basis concentrating on capital growth and when appropriate adopting an aggressive attitude to asset allocation and currency exposure.
SUMIT*	L	19.8	Capital growth by investing in unquoted companies, management buy-outs and management buy-ins where there are good prospects of realising the investment.
St Andrew	K	66.3	Investment in smaller companies in the UK and overseas.
St David's*	M	9.8(1)	Above average capital growth combined with a growing income by investing in UK growth stocks, recovery stocks, special situations and new issues.
S & P Linked (SPLIT)*	M	45.8	Fully invested in the following unit trusts: S & P Scotyields and S & P Investment Trust Units.

163

Investment trust	AITC cate-gory	Net assets £m	Investment objective
S & P Return of Assets (SPRAIT)*	A	53.7	Fully invested in the following unit trusts: 49.5% S & P High Return, 29% S & P Smaller Companies Income, 21.5% S & P American Income & Growth.
Saltire Insurance*	L	9.7	To invest in insurance and related services worldwide.
Schroder Global	D	84.4	Best overall return of capital and income in sterling terms through flexible global management.
Scottish American	A	228.9	Income and capital growth with a high proportion invested overseas and with emphasis on smaller companies.
Scottish & Mercantile	C	25.0	Capital growth.
Scottish Cities	C	22.0	Capital growth.
Scottish Eastern	D	360.0	Long-term capital growth through a geographically diversified portfolio.
Scottish Investment	D	450.7	High total return through an international portfolio of growth companies including unlisted companies where the prospects for growth justify the increased risk.
Scottish Mortgage	A	502.7	Maximum growth in both capital value and dividends.
Scottish National	M	265.4	To balance the long-term interests of income and capital shareholders by investing in higher-yielding UK equities, some convertibles and up to 20 per cent overseas.
Second Alliance	A	163.3	Steady growth of both income and capital.
Second Market*	D	13.6	Long-term capital growth primarily by investing in companies quoted on the second market of the French stock exchange.
Securities Trust of Scotland	J	206.1	Growth in income with a consequent increase in capital value.
Selective Assets	D	40.0(1)	Long-term capital growth in excess of the FT-Actuaries All Share Index by investing on a worldwide basis.
Shires	B	62.8	Invested principally in the UK in high yielding equities with up to a maximum of 25 per cent in unlisted investments.

Investment trust	AITC category	Net assets £m	Investment objective
Smaller Companies International	K	52.7	Long-term capital growth from a portfolio of small and medium sized companies.
Strata	K	18.7	Long-term capital growth by investing in smaller companies worldwide.
Stratton	D	18.3	Capital growth by investing internationally in a wide range of companies.
TR Australia	F	31.2	Long-term capital growth with reasonable income by investing predominantly in Australia with the balance in the UK.
TR City of London	B	170.6	Higher than average yield from a predominantly UK portfolio of quality stocks.
TR Industrial & General	A	612.6	To be flexible by investing anywhere in the world where income and capital growth can be achieved.
TR Natural Resources	H	80.9	Growth in total return through industrial specialisation in natural resources.
TR North America	E	62.2	Invested predominantly in North American companies considered to have substantial long-term potential for growth of capital and income.
TR Pacific	F	27.5	Capital growth by investing either directly or indirectly in Hong Kong, Malaysia, Singapore, Thailand, Philippines, South Korea, Taiwan, and as and when appropriate in other regional economies including Indonesia, and China.
TR Property	L	132.5	Invested mainly in property shares and property on an international basis.
TR Technology	I	320.9	Invested predominantly in companies significantly concerned with advanced technology. Partially unitised in the Spring of 1988.
TR Trustees	K	252.1	Long-term capital appreciation and increasing income by investing in a widely spread portfolio with the emphasis on smaller companies.
Temple Bar	B	155.4	To improve shareholders' total return.

Investment trust	AITC category	Net assets £m	Investment objective
Throgmorton Dual	M	30.8	To satisfy needs of both income and capital shareholders by investing primarily in higher-yielding smaller and medium-sized companies.
Throgmorton Trust	K	313.1	Emphasis on smaller companies entirely in the UK with special interest in newer growth industries.
Throgmorton USM	L	26.8	Capital growth by investing in USM companies.
Tor*	M	30.4(1)	To maintain a balanced portfolio with a reasonable geographical spread with minimum risk.
Tribune	D	114.2	Long-term capital growth through exposure to international markets.
Triplevest	M	102.8	Invested principally in UK securities, giving equal attention to both capital and income growth, reflecting the interest of both categories of shareholders.
Trust of Property Shares	L	6.9	Investing mainly in UK property companies and unlisted companies owning reversionary shop and office properties.
USDC	D	51.5	Long-term growth by investing in growth companies worldwide.
Updown	C	17.7	Increasing capital value of the portfolio while trying to maintain a reasonable rate of return.
Value & Income	L	29.9	Invested in UK high yielding property and smaller quoted companies designed to offer above average initial yield and growth prospects.
Vantage*	B	2.9	Long-term capital and income growth by investing principally in UK equities.
Viking Resources	H	28.8	Capital growth by investing in companies in the energy industry and in oil and gas-producing properties in the USA.
Whitbread*	L	235.6	To invest primarily in brewery companies.

166

Investment trust	AITC category	Net assets £m	Investment objective
Witan	A	527.4	To build up capital value of assets to provide a base for further income growth.
Yeoman	M	56.0	Invested for capital and income growth.

* = *not* members of AITC.
(I) = latest available figure.

APPENDIX 5 DIRECTORY OF MANAGEMENT COMPANIES

Self-managed investment trusts start on page 176.

AES Equity Ventures
Edmund House
12 Newall Street
Birmingham B3 3ER
Tel: 021-200 2244

Trust managed
SUMIT

Aberdeen Fund Managers
10 Queen's Terrace
Aberdeen AB9 1QJ
Tel: (0224) 631999

Trust managed
North of Scotland

Abingworth Management
Gillett House
55 Basinghall Street
London EC2V 5EA
Tel: 01-839 6745

Trust managed
Abingworth

Arbuthnot Fund Managers
131 Finsbury Pavement
London EC2A 1AY
Tel: 01-280 8583

Trust managed
Archimedes

Asset Managers
Queen's Chambers
2 North Street
Newport
Gwent NP9 1JZ
Tel: (0633) 244233

Trust managed
St David's

Baillie, Gifford
3 Glenfinlas Street
Edinburgh EH3 6YY
Tel: 031-225 2581

Trusts managed
Baillie Gifford Japan
Baillie Gifford Shin Nippon
Baillie Gifford Technology
Mid Wynd International
Monks
Scottish Mortgage

Bank in Liechtenstein (UK)
1 Devonshire Square
London EC2M 4UJ
Tel: 01-377 0404

Trust managed
German Securities

Baring Investment Management
8 Bishopsgate
London EC2N 4AE
Tel: 01-283 8833

Trusts managed
Stratton
Tribune

168

British Linen Fund Managers
32 Melville Street
Edinburgh EH3 7HA
Tel: 031-453 1919

Trust managed
Melville Street

CS Investments
125 High Holborn
London WC1V 6PY
Tel: 01-242 1148

Trusts managed
Children's Medical Charity
Group Development Capital

Capital Gearing Management
Royston House
34 Upper Queen Street
Belfast BT1 6HB
Tel: (0232) 244001

Trust managed
Capital Gearing

Certa Investment Management
6 Playhouse Yard
London EC4V 5EX
Tel: 01-489 0131

Trust managed
Multitrust

Chatsworth Management Services
4th Floor, Hesketh House
Portman Square
London W1H 0JR
Tel: 01-486 6351

Trust managed
Derby

City Financial Administration
20 Copthall Avenue
London EC2R 7PA
Tel: 01-623 2494

Trust managed
London & St Lawrence

Clayton Robard Management
c/o Tyndall Holdings
25 Bucklersbury
London EC4N 8TH
Tel: 01-248 3399

Trust managed
Australia

Discretionary Unit Fund Managers
5-9 Sun Street
London EC2M 2PS
Tel: 01-377 8819

Trust managed
Rights and Issues

Dunedin
Dunedin House
25 Ravelstone Terrace
Edinburgh EH4 3EX
Tel: 031-315 2500

Trusts managed
Dundee & London
Edinburgh Investment
First Scottish American
Northern American

Edinburgh Fund Managers
4 Melville Crescent
Edinburgh EH3 7JB
Tel: 031-226 4931

Trusts managed
American
Crescent Japan
EFM Dragon
New Tokyo
Smaller Companies International

Ely Place Investments
28 Ely Place
London EC1N 6RL
Tel: 01-242 0242

Trust managed
Primadona

169

Finsbury Asset Management
Neptune House
Triton Court
14 Finsbury Square
London EC2A 1BR
Tel: 01-256 8873

Trusts managed
Fashion & General
Lancashire & London
Scottish & Mercantile
Scottish Cities

**Fleming Investment
Trust Management**
25 Copthall Avenue
London EC2R 7DR
Tel: 01-638 5858

Trusts managed
Fleming American
Fleming Claverhouse
Fleming Enterprise
Fleming Far Eastern
Fleming Fledgeling
Fleming Japanese
Fleming Mercantile
Fleming Overseas
Fleming Technology
Fleming Universal

Foreign & Colonial Management
1 Laurence Pountney Hill
London EC4R 0BA
Tel: 01-623 4680

Trusts managed
F & C Enterprise
F & C Eurotrust
F & C Pacific
F & C Smaller Companies
Foreign and Colonial

**GT Management and
GT Venture Management**
8th Floor
8 Devonshire Square
London EC2M 4YJ
Tel: 01-283 2575

Trusts managed
Berry Starquest
GT Japan
GT Venture
Nordic
USDC

Gartmore Investment Management
Gartmore House
16-18 Monument Street
London EC3R 8QQ
Tel: 01-623 1212

Trusts managed
English & Caledonian
English & Scottish
Gartmore American Securities
Gartmore European
Gartmore Information & Financial
London & Strathclyde
Meldrum

Gartmore Scotland
Ashley House
181-195 West George Street
Glasgow G2 2HB
Tel: 041-248 3972

Trust managed
Scottish National

Glasgow Investment Managers
29 St Vincent Place
Glasgow G1 2DR
Tel: 041-226 4585

Trust managed
Shires

170

John Govett
Shackleton House
4 Battle Bridge Lane
London SE1 2HR
Tel: 01-378 7979

Trusts managed
Govett Atlantic
Govett Oriental
Govett Strategic

Grahams Rintoul
5-10 Bury Street
London EC3A 5AT
Tel: 01-623 8224

Trust managed
Grahams Rintoul

**Guinness Mahon Investment
Management**
32 St Mary at Hill
London EC3P 3AJ
Tel: 01-623 9333

Trust managed
Temple Bar

**Hambrecht & Quist Venture
Partners**
235 Montgomery Street
San Francisco
CA 94104
USA
Tel: (415) 576 3300

Trust managed
London American Ventures

Hambros Bank
41 Bishopsgate
London EC2P 2AA
Tel: 01-588 2851

Trusts managed
City of Oxford
Hambros

Henderson Administration
3 Finsbury Avenue
London EC2M 2PA
Tel: 01-638 5757

Trusts managed
British Kidney Patient
Electric & General
English National
Greenfriar
Lowland
Strata
Witan

Hodgson Martin
4A St Andrew Square
Edinburgh EH2 2BD
Tel: 031-557 3560

Trusts managed
New Darien
Saltire Insurance

**David Hume Investment
Management**
Empire House
123 Kennington Road
London SE11 6SF
Tel: 01-582 4030

Trust managed
Plantation

Ivory & Sime plc
1 Charlotte Square
Edinburgh EH2 4DZ
Tel: 031-225 1357

Trusts managed
Atlantic Assets
British Assets
Continental Assets
First Charlotte Assets
Independent
Investors Capital
Japan Assets
Pacific Assets
Personal Assets
Selective Assets
Viking Resources

**Kleinwort Grieveson Investment
Management**
10 Fenchurch Street
London EC3M 3LB
Tel: 01-623 8000

Trusts managed
Brunner
Jos Holdings
Kleinwort Charter
Kleinwort Overseas
Kleinwort Smaller Companies
Merchants

Kleinwort Development Capital
20 Fenchurch Street
London EC3P 3DB
Tel: 01-623 8000

Trust managed
Kleinwort Development

Laurwood
16 Buckingham Gate
London SW1E 6LB
Tel: 01-828 6123

Trust managed
British Empire Securities

Lazard Investors
21 Moorfields
London EC2P 2HT
Tel: 01-588 2721

Trusts managed
Raeburn
Romney

Lloyds Bank Fund Management
Elizabeth House
9-11 Bush Lane
London EC4P 4LN
Tel: 01-600 4500

Trusts managed
First Spanish
German Smaller Companies

**Lombard Odier International
Portfolio Management**
Norfolk House
13 Southampton Place
London WC1A 2AJ
Tel: 01-831 2350

Trust managed
Second Market

**Lombard Odier Investment
Management Services**
Norfolk House
13 Southampton Place
London WC1A 2AJ
Tel: 01-831 2350

Trust managed
Oceana

M & G
Three Quays
Tower Hill
London EC3R 6BQ
Tel: 01-626 4588

Trusts managed
External
M & G Dual
M & G Second Dual

MIM Limited
11 Devonshire Square
London EC2M 4YR
Tel: 01-626 3434

Trusts managed
City & Commercial
Consolidated Venture
Drayton Consolidated
Drayton Far Eastern
Drayton Japan
English & International
Fundinvest
Triplevest

Martin Currie Investment Management
29 Charlotte Square
Edinburgh EH2 4HA
Tel: 031-225 3811

Trusts managed
Martin Currie Pacific
St Andrew
Scottish Eastern
Securities Trust of Scotland

Maunby Investment Management
4 Mount Parade
Harrogate
North Yorkshire HG1 1BX
Tel: (0423) 523553

Trust managed
Fulcrum

Merchant Navy Investment Management
30 Finsbury Circus
London EC2M 5QQ
Tel: 01-588 6000

Trusts managed
CDFC
Clydesdale
Ensign

Mercury Asset Management
33 King William Street
London EC4R 9AS
Tel: 01-280 2800

Trust managed
Keystone

Morgan Grenfell Trust Managers
46 New Broad Street
London EC2M 1NB
Tel: 01-256 7500

Trusts managed
Anglo & Overseas
Overseas

Murray Johnstone
7 West Nile Street
Glasgow G1 2PX
Tel: 041-226 3131

Trusts managed
Murray Electronics
Murray Income
Murray International
Murray Smaller Markets
Murray Technology
Murray Ventures

Olayan Europe
9 Upper Belgrave Street
London SW1X 8BD
Tel: 01-235 4802

Trust managed
General Consolidated

Panfida Managers
James House
1 Babmaes Street
London SW1Y 6HD
Tel: 01-925 0555

Trust managed
'Investing in Success'

Paribas Asset Management (UK)
PO Box 216
Garrard House
31-45 Gresham Street
London EC2V 7LH
Tel: 01-600 4177

Trust managed
Paribas French

River & Mercantile Investment Management
7 Lincoln's Inn Fields
London WC2A 3BP
Tel: 01-405 7722

Trusts managed
River & Mercantile
River & Mercantile American
River & Mercantile Geared

Rivermoor Management Services
Friendly House
21-24 Chiswell Street
London EC1Y 4TU
Tel: 01-628 5653

Trusts managed
Danae
Jove

J Rothschild Investment Management
15 St James's Place
London SW1A 1NW
Tel: 01-493 8111

Trust managed
Precious Metals

N M Rothschild Asset Management
Five Arrows House
St Swithin's Lane
London EC4NP 8NR
Tel: 01-280 5000

Trust managed
Equity Consort

Save & Prosper Group
1 Finsbury Avenue
London EC2M 2QY
Tel: 01-588 1717

Trusts managed
Save & Prosper Linked
Save & Prosper Return of Assets

Schroder Investment Management
36 Old Jewry
London EC2R 8BS
Tel: 01-382 6000

Trust managed
Schroder Global

Stewart Ivory
45 Charlotte Square
Edinburgh EH2 4HW
Tel: 031-226 3271

Trust managed
Scottish American

Stewart OLIM
Pollen House
10-12 Cork Street
London W1X 1PD
Tel: 01-439 4400

Trust managed
Value & Income

TAI Securities
St Andrew's House
40 Broadway
London SW1H 0BT
Tel: 01-222 5496

Trust managed
Continental & Industrial

Tarbutt & Company
Knightsbridge House
197 Knightsbridge
London SW7 1RB
Tel: 01-225 1044

Trusts managed
River Plate
Vantage

Thornton Management
15th Floor
33 Cavendish Square
London W1M 7HF
Tel: 01-493 7262

Trusts managed
Child Health Research
Marine Adventure Sailing

3i Portfolio Management
91 Waterloo Road
London SE1 8XP
Tel: 01-928 7822

Trusts managed
London Atlantic
North British Canadian

**Throgmorton Investment
Management Services**
Royal London House
22-25 Finsbury Square
London EC2A 1DS
Tel: 01-374 4100

Trusts managed
Alva
New Throgmorton (1983)
Throgmorton Dual
Throgmorton Trust
Throgmorton USM

Top Technology
21-22 Tooks Court
Cursitor Street
London EC4A 1LB
Tel: 01-242 9900

Trust managed
Hambros Advanced Technology

Touche, Remnant
Mermaid House
2 Puddle Dock
London EC4V 3AT
Tel: 01-236 6565

Trusts managed
Bankers'
Law Debenture Corporation
TR Australia
TR City of London
TR Industrial & General
TR Natural Resources
TR North America
TR Pacific
TR Property
TR Technology
TR Trustee

SELF-MANAGED INVESTMENT TRUSTS

Albany
Port of Liverpool Building
Pier Head
Liverpool L3 1NW
Tel: 051-236 8674

Alliance Trust
Meadow House
64 Reform Street
Dundee DD1 1TJ
Tel: (0382) 21234

Ambrose
London International Press Centre
76 Shoe Lane
London EC4A 3JB
Tel: 01-583 4690

Bertrams
Victoria House
Vernon Place
London SW1B 4DH
Tel: 01-242 9452

British Investment
46 Castle Street
Edinburgh EH2 3BR
Tel: 031-225 2348

CSC
Sheffield House
29 Boltro Road
Haywards Heath
Sussex RH16 1BW
Tel: (0444) 459316

Candover Investments
Cedric House
8-9 East Harding Street
London EC4A 3AS
Tel: 01-583 5090

Electra
65 Kingsway
London WC2B 6QT
Tel: 01-831 6464

English & Caledonian
E & C Management
Gartmore House
16-18 Monument Street
London EC3R 8AJ
Tel: 01-623 1212

Globe
Electra House
Temple Place
London WC2R 3HP
Tel: 01-836 7766

Gresham House
24 Austin Friars
London EC2N 2EN
Tel: 01-588 7352

Jersey General
PO Box 1
35 Don Street
St Helier
Jersey
Channel Islands
Tel: (0534) 21381

Majedie
Plantation House
10-15 Mincing Lane
London EC3M 3LS
Tel: 01-626 1243

Mezzanine
23 Cathedral Yard
Exeter EX1 1HB
Tel: (0392) 412122

Moorgate
9 Upper Belgrave Street
London SW1X 8BD
Tel: 01-235 4802

Practical Investment
Room 333
Dunster House
Mark Lane
London EC3R 7AR
Tel: 01-623 8893

Scottish Investment
6 Albyn Place
Edinburgh EH2 4NL
Tel: 031-225 7781

Second Alliance
Meadow House
64 Reform Street
Dundee DD1 1TJ
Tel: (0382) 21234

Tor
6 Caer Street
Swansea SA1 3PS
Tel: (0792) 52037

Trust of Property Shares
6 Welbeck Street
London W1M 8BS
Tel: 01-486 4684

Updown
12 Tokenhouse Yard
London EC2R 7AN
Tel: 01-588 2828

Welsh Industrial
24 Austin Friars
London EC2N 2EN
Tel: 01-588 7352

Whitbread Investment
Brewery
Chiswell Street
London EC1Y 4SD
Tel: 01-606 4455

Yeoman
11 Devonshire Square
London EC2M 4YR
Tel: 01-626 3434

GLOSSARY

ACCOUNT The dealing period on London's International Stock Exchange. When you buy and sell shares you do so during an account, which normally lasts a fortnight. If you are buying shares, you only have to hand your money over on the account settlement day which is normally ten days after the end of the account. Likewise when you sell shares, you only get paid on the settlement day following the account in which you made your transaction. Dealing on account is the high-risk practice of buying more shares than you can afford in the hope that they go up during the account period and you can sell them for a profit before the end of the account. Not recommended.

'B' SHARES These are shares attached to certain investment trusts which receive an annual bonus issue of 'B' shares instead of a dividend. Investment trusts with 'B' shares were an alternative to split level investment trusts, until a tax ruling removed their attraction. They are now virtually redundant.

BACK-TO-BACK LOAN The practice of borrowing money in a foreign currency and matching it with a UK deposit. This is often achieved by borrowing money in the local currency of an overseas company and matching the loan by depositing sterling with the same company's UK subsidiary. Back-to-back loans don't count as borrowings. They are used as a method of minimising exchange rate risk. They are especially popular with unit trusts, which are not permitted to borrow money, but they are also used by investment trusts.

BALANCE SHEET The annual statement of a company's assets and liabilities. An investment trust balance sheet shows how much the trust has invested, and how much it has borrowed.

BARGAIN Nothing to do with value for money. This is a stock market jargon word meaning an instruction to buy or sell shares.

BETA RATIO A way of measuring a particular share's volatility — or how much the share price can be expected to rise and fall in relation to a given stock market index.

BID PRICE Market makers (q.v.) earn their living from the spread between the price they are willing to buy shares at and the price they are willing to pay for them. The price they are willing to pay for them — or bid for them — is called the bid price. This is the price you get when you sell shares.

BIG BANG The City revolution of October 1986, when the Stock Exchange abandoned its fixed commission rate and age old prohibition which prevented stockbrokers from acting as jobbers and making a market in company securities and Government stocks. See MARKET MAKER.

BONUS ISSUE A free issue of shares. If, for example, a company does a one-for-two bonus issue, shareholders get one new share for every two they already own. In theory, the share price should adjust itself downwards to take account of the increased number of shares in issue. But quite often a bonus issue acts as fillip to the overall share price. Also known as a scrip issue.

BREAK-UP VALUE The value of an investment trust after deducting the redemption value of all the prior charges. This is the method normally used in investment trust accounts.

CAPITAL SHARE A type of share issued by split capital investment trusts which is entitled to all the capital from the trust's investments but none of the income. Particularly suitable for higher rate taxpayers.

CHARTS A method of predicting the future price movements of a share by looking at a chart of the share's previous price behaviour and looking for certain patterns.

COMMISSION The charge levied by a stockbroker for buying and selling shares. For small shareholders, commission is generally 1.65 per cent, but is usually subject to a minimum of between £10 and £50.

CONVERTIBLE LOAN STOCK A fixed interest investment which can be converted into ordinary shares at a price fixed in advance. The initial yield on convertible loan stock is higher than on the ordinary shares.

CURRENCY HEDGING The practice of trying to eliminate exchange rate risk from a portfolio of shares invested overseas. The most common method is to borrow money in the currency in which the money is to be invested. But other methods include buying currency forward, i.e. buying it tomorrow at today's price, and using financial futures.

DEBENTURE STOCK A fixed interest stock issued by companies, including investment trusts, which pays a fixed amount of interest until it is repaid. Debenture stock has a charge on the company's assets. If a company goes bust, the debenture stockholders are first in line to be repaid before the loan and preference stockholders and equity shareholders.

DISCOUNT The gap between the price at which an investment trust share changes hands on the stock market and the value of its underlying investments. Most investment trusts stand at a discount to their net asset value.

DISGUISED RIGHTS ISSUE The practice whereby an industrial company raises money by taking over an investment trust and paying for it with its own shares. The investment trust's portfolio of shares is then turned into cash which the company can use for its own purpose.

DIVIDEND The income which a company pays its shareholders. Investment trusts are required to pay virtually all their income to shareholders as dividends.

DUAL CAPITAL TRUST See SPLIT CAPITAL.

EQUITY Another word for company shares, including preference shares.

FT ACTUARIES ALL-SHARE INDEX The most comprehensive of all the UK stock market indexes. It comprised 720 shares at the beginning of 1988 with 40 subsections including one investment trusts. Comprising 87. Worked out once a day.

FT-SE 100 INDEX An index of 100 leading UK shares, worked out continuously throughout the day. Traded options and financial futures contracts linked to the movement of UK shares are generally based on this index.

FT INDUSTRIAL ORDINARY SHARE INDEX Usually called the FT Ordinary or the 30-Share Index it is still the most widely quoted UK stock market index, but because it is made up of only 30 stocks, it is not always thought to give a true picture of how the market is moving. It is worked out every hour.

FIXED INTEREST SECURITIES A security which pays a fixed rate of interest. The term covers debenture and loan stocks, and preference shares, as well as Government stocks and local authority bonds.

FRANKED INCOME Dividends from UK ordinary and preference shares are referred to as franked income because they are paid net of basic rate tax. Because tax has already been paid, there is no extra corporation tax to pay when they are received by an investment trust.

FUTURES A financial contract which gives you the right to buy or sell something in the future at a price determined today. Used extensively for commodities such as coffee, cocoa, copper and tin, but there are now futures contracts covering such things as foreign currencies, Government bonds, even the FT-SE 100 Index.

GEARING This is when an investment trust borrows money to increase its exposure to equity markets. A geared investment trust will rise faster in rising markets, and fall faster in falling markets.

180

GEARING FACTOR A measurement of gearing. The percentage by which an investment trust's net assets per share would rise if its investments doubled in value.

GENERAL TRUST The traditional investment trust which aims to combine capital and income growth by investing anywhere in the world. Sometimes called generalist trusts.

GOING CONCERN BASIS A method of calculating investment trust net assets using the market value rather than the repayment or redemption price of any prior charges.

HEDGING See CURRENCY HEDGING.

INCOME SHARE A type of share issued by split capital investment trusts which is entitled to all the income from the trust's investments, but none of the capital.

INDEPENDENT INVESTMENT TRUST An investment trust which employs its own managers, and doesn't employ a separate management company.

LEVERAGE See GEARING.

LIMITED LIFE TRUST See WINDING UP DATE.

LISTED INVESTMENTS Securities listed on a recognised stock exchange.

LOAN STOCK A fixed interest investment paying a regular income for a fixed number of years, and traded on the stock market. Investment trusts rarely issue loan stock these days; however, there are still a large number of investment trust loan stocks quoted on the stock market.

MANAGEMENT CHARGE The amount deducted from a unit trust or investment trust to cover the cost of managing it. Investment trust management charges are normally less than those charged by unit trusts.

MANAGEMENT COMPANY A company employed to manage an investment trust. Many management companies look after a whole range of investment and unit trusts.

MARKET CAPITALISATION How much the company is worth on the stock market. The value is calculated by multiplying all the shares in issue by the share price.

MARKET MAKER The organisation which fixes the price of a particular share taking into account supply and demand. Before Big Bang, only jobbers were permitted to make a market in company shares. Now stockbrokers can do so, although the two activities — that of making a market in shares and dealing with clients — must be kept separate if they both go on within the same firm of stockbrokers.

MARKET VALUE The same as market capitalisation.

MARKETABILITY Some shares are easier to buy and sell than others. The International Stock Exchange divides shares into four categories — alpha, beta, gamma and delta — depending on their marketability. Alpha stocks are extremely easy to buy and sell, delta stocks are the least readily marketable.

MIDDLE PRICE The share price normally quoted in the newspapers. It is pitched half-way between the price at which you can buy and sell them. See **BID PRICE** and **OFFER PRICE**.

NET ASSET VALUE A company's assets less its liabilities. In the case of an investment trust, it is the value of its investments less its liabilities, including any borrowings.

NET ASSETS PER SHARE The above figure divided by the number of shares in issue. Net assets per share are often referred to as fully diluted. This is the figure taking into account any shares which may be issued following conversion by warrant or convertible loan stockholders.

NEW TIME On the last afternoon of the Stock Exchange account you can buy shares in what is known as 'new time', effectively carrying your deal over into the next account.

OFFER PRICE The price the market maker is prepared to sell shares — or offer them — is called the offer price and it's the price you pay when you buy shares. See **BID PRICE**.

ORDINARY SHARE When you buy an ordinary share you are buying a share in that company and you become a part owner. If the company does well, its price will rise to reflect that success. If, on the other hand, the company is unsuccessful and fails you risk losing all your money.

OVER-THE-COUNTER MARKET Share dealers buy and sell shares privately on what is called the over-the-counter market, where buyers are usually matched with sellers. Tread with caution. Many shares traded on share dealers' own over-the-counter markets can be difficult to sell, because of this necessity to find a buyer for the shares you are selling.

PEP Stands for Personal Equity Plan. A Government-sponsored scheme which allows investors to invest up to £3,000 (in 1988) in company shares free of income tax and capital gains tax, so long as they are held for at least a year. PEPs directly into unit trusts or investment trusts are restricted to £500 a year (in 1988) or a quarter if held in conjunction with a scheme directly invested in shares.

PREFERENCE SHARE A fixed interest investment with no fixed date on which it is to be repaid and where the dividend continues to be paid for as long as the trust stays in existence, or the shares are repaid. Preference shares form part of a company's share capital, but shareholders' rights are limited compared to those of the ordinary shareholders. However, if the company fails preference shareholders are paid out ahead of ordinary shareholders.

PREMIUM The percentage by which a trust's share price exceeds its net assets per share. Few investment trusts stand at a premium. See DISCOUNT.

PRIOR CHARGES Liabilities such as debenture and loan stocks which take precedence over ordinary shares in a company winding up or liquidation.

PROSPECTUS A weighty document put out by a company when it seeks a listing for its shares, or when it is raising fresh funds with a rights issue.

REINVESTMENT OF DIVIDENDS A facility offered by a number of investment trusts and unit trusts which automatically invests the net dividend in further shares or units.

RIGHTS ISSUE A method companies use to raise money from their existing shareholders, by offering them the chance to buy new shares, usually at a discount. Shareholders are free to turn down the offer.

SECONDARY MARKETS Second tier stock markets used by small and emerging companies. The French and Japanese stock markets both have well-developed secondary markets. The USM market (q.v.) is our equivalent to these secondary markets.

SETTLEMENT The date, usually ten days after the end of the stock exchange account, when you pay for any shares you have bought during the account, and likewise the date when your stockbroker pays you for any shares you have sold.

SCRIP ISSUE See BONUS ISSUE.

SHARPE RATIO A way of measuring share price performance. Sharpe ratios are an indication of the likely reward from a given level of risk. This measurement leads you to trusts whose past performance has combined above average performance with below average volatility. Sharpe ratios are named after Professor William Sharpe.

SHORT SELLING Selling shares you do not own in the hope that the price falls before the end of the account. Not recommended for the private investor.

SPLIT CAPITAL Split capital investment trusts normally have two classes of shares — income and capital. The capital shares benefit from all the capital growth, but get no income. The income shares receive all the dividend income but none of the capital gain. Also called split level, dual capital, or dual purpose investment trusts.

STOCKBROKER An organisation which buys and sells stock market investments on behalf of investment clients who may be private individuals, big City institutions or corporations. Since Big Bang stockbrokers have also been able to make a market in shares. See MARKET MAKER.

STUDS This stands for Stepped Interest Debenture Stocks. These are debenture stocks where the interest payment starts low and increases year by year until it reaches a predetermined level.

TAX CREDIT UK companies pay their dividends with an amount for the basic rate of tax deducted at source. When you receive a dividend voucher, the amount of tax deducted is shown as a tax credit. If you don't pay tax, you can reclaim the tax credit from the Inland Revenue.

THIRD MARKET Part of the International Stock Exchange, the Third Market exists to help new and emerging companies to raise money and have their shares quoted. For the private investor, third market shares are a high risk investment.

TOTAL ASSETS The value of an investment trust's portfolio before deducting any liabilities, including borrowings.

TRADED OPTION Similar to a futures contract, a traded option gives you the right to buy or sell something in the future at a price fixed today. Traded options are available on a number of shares as well as on the FT-SE 100 Index.

UNDERWRITING For a fee, the big City institutions agree to mop up any shares not taken up during a rights issue, a new share issue, or a privatisation.

UNIT TRUST A collective investment scheme. Investors buy units in a fund whose price reflects the value of the underlying investments. Unit trusts are open-ended. The number of units in issue depends on the number of people who want them, contracting and expanding to meet demand.

UNLISTED SECURITIES MARKET (USM) The International Stock Exchange's second tier market. Smaller companies wanting the advantages of a quotation for their shares without the expense of a full Stock Exchange listing can opt for the USM.

WARRANT Warrants are issued by companies themselves, and they are particularly popular with investment trusts. Warrants give their holders the right to buy the ordinary shares at a predetermined price at some time in the future.

WINDING UP DATE Some investment trusts have fixed dates on which they are to be wound up and the assets returned to shareholders. Most split capital investment trusts normally have a winding up date.

YIELD The annual gross dividend payment expressed as a percentage of the share price.

ZERO DIVIDEND PREFERENCE SHARE A preference share which pays no dividend, but where the income rolls up in the capital value instead.

INDEX

British Airports Authority, 3
British Airways, 3,36
British Assets, 13,84,89
British Gas, 3,36
British Investment Trust, 43,89
British Rail Pension Fund, 15
British Steamship Investment
    Trust, 44
British Telecom, 3,36,40
Building society
  buying shares through, 40
  deposit income, 9,72
  emergency fund deposited with, 2
  performance, 2
Burton, 52
Business Expansion Scheme funds,
   47
Buying
  methods, 36,40-41
  savings schemes, 36
  source of advice, 39-40
  stockbroker, use of, *see*
    Stockbroker
  unit trust and investment trust
    compared, 32-33
  warrants, 64-65

Candover, 30
Capital gains tax, 11,74,121
Capital growth, 72
Capital value of investment, 9
Carless Capel & Leonard, 122
Cedar Trust, 15,123
Chairman's statement, 96-97
Chart Analysis, 89-90
Charter, 84
Charts, 79,89-90
Cheltenham & Gloucester, 40
Choice of investment trust, 71-74,
   78-79
City of Edinburgh, Life Assurance
   Company, 110
Closed-end fund, 29
Cochrane, Grant, 83
Commission
  James Capel, 38
  stockbroker, 1,37,38
Company
  corporate structure, 9-11
  shares compared with investment
    trust shares, 8-9

Complacency of investment trusts,
   1-2
Consolidated Venture, 82
Consols, 52
Continental Union Gas Companies,
   13
Convertible loan stocks, 54
Corporate structure
  pros and cons, 9-10
  regulatory restrictions, 10-11
  shareholder power, 10
Corporation tax, 11
Costs
  advice, 38-39
  dealing, 38
Courtaulds, 8
Crescent Japan, 45,46,81-82
Criminal offence
  failure to register, 10

Daily Telegraph, 105,107
Dealing in shares, 3-4,38
Debenhams, 40
Debenture stocks
  borrowings, 53-54
  gearing through, 26-27
  stepped interest, 16-17,26
Department of Trade and Industry,
   see Trade and Industry,
   Department of
Directors' report, 98
Discounts
  danger of, 20
  fluctuation, 19-20
  history, 20,22
  meaning, 19
  narrowing, 20
  performance as guide, 86-87
  reading, 22,25
  threat from, 14-15
  warrant, 63
  widening, 19-20
Disguised rights issues, 15-16, 122
Dividends
  after-tax, 11
  companies and investment trusts
    compared, 8
  increasing, 9
  tax credit offset against, 11
Double taxation, 11
Drapers Gardens, 41